THE
POSTMAN

MARC ROSSON

Burning Bulb

PUBLISHING

The Postman
By **Marc Rosson**

Burning Bulb Publishing
P.O. Box 4721
Bridgeport, WV 26330-4721
United States of America
www.BurningBulbPublishing.com

First Edition.

Paperback Edition ISBN: 978-1-964172-54-5

Preface

This book is dedicated to the mail carriers and first responders, past, present, and future.

For many people, the mail carrier may be the only person they may see in a day. For many others, the last person they see in this world is their mail carrier or a first responder. I have spent about 16 years delivering mail. I have family members and friends who have also delivered mail. I was a volunteer firefighter, first responder for several years, and then the fire chief for 5 of those years in the same community I grew up in.

Through my time doing this, I had a passenger with me; it was God. He has the best advice and guidance; you just have to listen.

I started writing this book in 2017, but started over and got serious about it in 2025. As I was writing it, friends and family would say, "Don't forget to put this story in," or, "Do you remember this?" Everything in this book, I have seen, but some are written from the perspective of those family members and friends. There are many more stories I could put in, but a person can only laugh so much.

God be with you.
–Marc Rosson

Chapter 1

It wasn't that Marcos didn't enjoy being a postman. He did. He just didn't like doing it six days a week with no replacement or break.

Vacations were a distant dream, schedules were his ball-and-chain, fastening him to set hours that couldn't be stiffer if it were carved in stone. Every day he got behind the wheel of his vehicle, he juggled a mixture of enjoying his job with the dread of never seeing an end in sight.

As with every job, there were pros and cons to everything. The pros? He got to drive around his favorite small town, say hello to people he'd known forever and loved as he handed off their dreaded bills, junk magazines, and packages. In a small, tight-knit community, it occurred to him on more than one occasion that he was, perhaps, the only person they might see or talk to in a day. People like Mrs. Henderson, or the lonely man down that ill-maintained country road, who spent endless hours interacting with the television or tending their garden as their escape from solitude. To think that he might be the ray of sunshine in their day, something they looked forward to, even if it was just a five-minute human interaction, was an honor for him.

The other pro he could think of was something a little more personal to him. He was usually done in the afternoon and had the rest of the late day and evening to himself. To get caught up on other things that fell behind while he was at work. So really, the second pro led into his list of cons.

He never got a break.

That's right. Heavy rain, tornadoes, wind, scorching heat, road construction, and all, the community still depended on him to bring them their bills and junk mail. People in America couldn't survive with a five-day mail route, oh, no. They needed it delivered six days a week, leaving Marcos the seventh as his only day to just be himself. And even then, he was still running, although going to church wasn't quite as mentally taxing as address-to-address.

Marcos took a breath and leaned back in the pew as the pastor drew the service to a close, one fine Sunday morning. Calling out a hymn number, he bid the congregation to rise and join him in a final song of worship. Marcos rose to his feet along with all the other members of his congregation, chiding himself for letting his mind run adrift with work-related matters rather than taking copious notes on 1 John chapter 3. Today, of all days, he had an excuse to sit back, relax, and enjoy his day of rest and not get so caught up in the drain of knowing that he had six days stretching ahead of him with little to no break. And why was that?

Marcos couldn't help but hint at a smile as he opened the hymnbook to the designated number. This week would be sprinkled with excitement. He was training a replacement. Maybe not someone to fully take his place, but someone to alleviate the pressure of having to be at work any time the doors were open. He could hardly believe it. After all this time, he had finally broken down and requested that someone else fill the front seat of the mail delivery vehicle, and be the one to take the brunt of the dogs, the people angry for bringing letters from the IRS and not delivering their packages exactly at 8:00 am. While Marcos could sit back and focus on other things, such as being at home. Maybe re-memorizing what some of the rooms inside his house looked like. Yet even with the hope of a new trainee, he hesitated. He'd been in the field long enough to know how these things worked. You could either wind up with a gem of an employee – punctual, cheerful, a great learner, and fluent in initiative – or you could wind up with the other side. *Sorry, I'm late. Overslept. I can't wait to go home already, and it's only 8:02 am. Do I have to deliver all this mail? What do I do next?*

This wasn't the first replacement he'd trained. And too many of them had that same attitude of the latter. Marcos could hear it now. And while he hoped that he was getting a good one, the Russian Roulette

---

wouldn't be solved until tomorrow, when he'd find out who he was dealing with.

The congregation sang the final note, bowed their heads to the final prayer, and then did what all small-town churches did. High-tail it out of the sanctuary as if their lunch was getting cold. Then, proceeded to stand around in the parking lot for one final meet-and-greet before jumping in the car to get to their Sunday roasts. Marcos enjoyed the fellowship after church. Even when the humidity hung thick in the air, as it did today, he loved taking the time to talk to the congregation members. To him, they were family, as was every member of this small town to a certain point. Yes, even the mean ones. Every family has one or two black sheep, right?

He shook the pastor's hand and headed out the door, only to spot Leon standing just outside. "What's going on, brother?" Marcos greeted cheerfully, garnering a look over the older man's shoulder.

Leon's eyes lit with recognition. He shifted his Bible to his left hand to tuck it against his torso as he extended a hand out to Marcos. "Not much, man, how are you doing?"

Marcos shook the proffered hand. Enthusiasm oozed from him as his voice rose to the charismatic level of cheerful greeting he was known for. "Oh, another day, another week. You been doing all right?"

"Hanging in there. The rains nearly washed out my garden, but I got a fresh row of beans sprouting. I'm waiting on the tomatoes to ripen up, so I can take them to the Farmer's Market."

Marcos smiled. While his own Southern accent thickened his words, Leon's held more of the deep south drawl, adding an endearing *er* at the end of *tomato*. "They say it's supposed to start drying out. I'll believe it when I see it."

The two men realized at the same time how they were clogging traffic behind them with their conversation, and stepped to the side. As the members filtered out, the talk of garden shifted to something else as Livy exited the church. She greeted Marcos with the same quiet cheer that she brightened his day with. Beside her, her best friend, Hallie, hobbled along beside her. The two older women could start a quilting group if they wanted to, and still have a fun time if it was just them. Marcos wasn't sure how long they'd known each other, but they went so far back, he doubted even they knew.

"I heard they got you a replacement, finally!" Hallie announced with as much cheer as Marcos felt, though perhaps a little more faith. "Is the new fellow starting tomorrow?"

"Yep, he sure is." Marcos nodded, his mind switching gears back to his earlier thoughts as they closed the service. "It's time for me to have a break."

Livy's eager nod reflected that she understood. Like Marcos, she was a hard worker who knew no days off except Sunday. Retirement was within reach of her weathered fingers, but she hadn't quite taken that plunge, yet. "Well," a small chuckle preceded her answer. "Just remember to have patience with him. Don't go running him off, now. You *need* a break!"

Running him off? Never! Marcos might scare him a little bit, all the while with a smile on his face. But if the fellow chose to leave, that was on him. It was up to him if he could take it or not. If he pushed through, great. If not? Well, at least Marcos could say that he'd trained him well. He didn't mention that to Livy, however. Just laughed right along with her because everyone present – Leon, Livy, Hallie, himself – knew Marcos well enough to know that Livy's statement was far more than just a tease. It was more of a gentle suggestion, masked in a tease. "I won't run him off. What are you talking about?" They shared some easy laughter and Marcos ended on a sigh. "Yep, I know. Six days a week hurts."

"Oh, I know it." Hallie raised her eyebrows, wearily. "They got you working to death."

"You ain't kidding," Marcos replied with a chuckle. "Well, I just hope they send me somebody good."

"Wouldn't count on it!" Leon broke into some laughter.

Marcos chuckled, bantering easy with the group. "Thanks for the encouragement."

He spent some time catching up on Leon's garden, Hallie's grandchildren and Livy's most recent job's bullet points before they departed for the rest of their quiet day. Marcos slid into the front seat of his vehicle, put it in drive and headed through the thickly forested road back home again. The haze in the air told him that the humidity was sticking around for a while, another reminder that this week was going to be nothing short of mentally whitewater rafting. It was easy to fall into Leon and Livy's doubt about the guy they'd hired for the postal service. Marcos would spend the rest of the week – perhaps longer – coaching a new mind how to do his job. The thought concerned him, only slightly. Would the kid do it right? What happened when Marcos had finished his training and turned him loose behind the wheel for the first time, a tote full of mail and a brain full of the mail route? What would happen? No one liked getting someone else's mail, and they liked it even less when the neighbor in the next town over received theirs. Especially the important letters.

But if Marcos didn't get him a replacement soon so he could take a breather, then perhaps the same thing would start to happen anyway. Marcos was meticulous. He read every numerical on the address twice, to avoid mistakes like delivering an article of mail to 345 instead of 354. Memorized each name, organized it fittingly in his tote beside him to ride for the day. Knew everyone along his mail route and was quite familiar with each preference and quirk they allotted him. That didn't mean that fatigue wouldn't get in there and mess something up, however.

He pulled into his driveway, determined not to think about it anymore. After all, it would be fine! He was worried for nothing. It was delivering mail in a small town, population 1,000 if they were generous.

What could go wrong?

Chapter 2

Sunday evening bled into Sunday night, and before Marcos knew it, he was awakened by the familiar sound of his alarm, slapping him out of his weekend mode and into the work week ahead. He rose to the side of the bed, muscles stiff from relaxing all night. A simple stretched jarred them awake as he robotically set about his morning routine. First, to drag himself out of bed. Always the first step to overcoming the temptation to get back into it. Nearly the first thought that greeted him when he opened his eyes was the reminder of what this day held.

Today, he was meeting and training someone new.

The pep talk he'd given himself Sunday morning was all but forgotten as he shuffled through his morning routine. He even tried humming an upbeat song, the music that had been stuck in his head since last night. He tugged on his boots, which always gave him a ready feeling to combat anything. Dogs nipping at his ankles, snakes hiding under porches, no matter what, the cowboy boots made him invincible.

He mechanically went about brushing his teeth and hair, counting down the minutes in his head before he had to walk out that door and into a brand new day. Once finished, he strode into the kitchen where his regular routine of making coffee awaited him. He didn't switch on a coffee pot like most people. Marcos took his coffee-making very seriously. The first thing to do was roast the beans, then grind the beans into powder, which is exactly what he did. The finer the powder, the stronger the taste and hopefully, the caffeine jolt.

As he set about methodically pouring his coffee grounds into the maker, he heated the water in the same pot where the beans had been roasting. People who used the same coffee filters, the same coffee pot, day in and day out, were missing out.

The coffee took too long to brew, as it usually did, tempting him with the smell of the brewing caffeine jolt he needed. *Come on, coffee.* He consolidated the water and roasted beans into the coffee pot, then turned it on. Something had to get him through this day. Marcos spent his time mentally swinging between an eagerness to meet the new face so he could start the countdown to his vacation and dreading having to hold someone's hand while he tried to do his own workload for the day.

With a final series of growls, the coffee pot announced that it was done brewing. Marcos poured the contents into a cup big enough to last him a couple of hours and grabbed everything else he needed. The birds were already awakened, singing cheerfully enough to bring a smile to his face as he slipped into the driver's seat of his personal vehicle and started the engine. He slipped his faithful companion – the coffee cup – into the cup holder and fastened his seat belt before putting the car in drive. He tuned in to the Gospel song, jamming out a good morning to God on his radio and hummed along with it. In the end, he decided the Gospel song was better than the caffeine jolt he sipped from his coffee cup.

The miles between him and the post office shortened, and before he knew it, he was urging his car up the ill-maintained hill that led to his work headquarters and angling the car into the parking lot. With a final hum, the engine went to sleep until he needed it, later.

Marcos grabbed his coffee and everything else he needed, slipping out the door. His boots hit the post office's parking lot one by one.

Another day, another week. Let's see what this day brings.

The humidity was so thick, you could taste it. Heavy enough to bring the cicadas to life early. Marcos gauged the day's temperature by the moisture in the air. Looked like it was going to be another scorcher, so thank goodness for the AC in the vehicle. All around him, the town was starting to perk to life. The nighttime quiet was driven away by the work trucks rumbling up and down the road and cars taking the curve by the post office too fast, as they always did.

He closed the car door behind him, silently reminding himself of his mantra the previous night. *I'm going to teach him the best I can. What could go wrong? This'll be fun.*

On one hand, it was a good thing. Training a replacement meant another body in the office, so Marcos could take a day off once in a while. But on the other hand, for all he knew, he could be stuck with someone fresh out of high school, who only knew the word *mail* from words like *Email* or *Instamail.* Marcos didn't want to be teaching his replacement what a stamp was in addition to the mail route.

He left the humidity behind, trading the sticky atmosphere for the stale scent of paper and stamps. The door to the post office closed behind him, sealing him inside long enough to gather the mail.

The clerk, Lizzy, had already taken her place behind the counter, prepping for the day ahead. Armed with a cup of coffee of her own on the table and a determined smile, she looked ready to take on the world for the rest of her shift.

"Good morning, Lizzy," Marcos greeted her cheerfully.

"Good morning," she returned with a smile.

Marcos glanced around the claustrophobic space. Of course, he and Lizzy were the only ones here. What happened to the days of showing up ten minutes early to a new job, or you were considered late? Guess they didn't teach that anymore, either. "Where's the new guy?"

"You're early." Lizzy's lips curved with the laughter she sprinkled into her tone.

Early! That was no excuse. Marcos chuckled a bit in acknowledgment.

"And be nice!" Lizzy wagged her finger at him. Her lips creased with laughter. "Don't tell him it's terrible. Let him get broken in, and then make his own determination."

Marcos snorted a laugh. Of course he would be nice! Being honest *was* being nice. Better to prepare someone for the real world than to sugar-coat it and let the bitterness surprise them when all the sugar dissolved.

"Besides. You need a break." Lizzy continued making her case as she turned on her computer for the day. That old dinosaur usually took several minutes to boot, so the new guy wasn't the only thing running behind today.

Marcos couldn't deny Lizzy's statement. He did need a break. That's why he was doing this. "Okay."

Lizzy calmed her tone. "His name is James, by the way. And he's from Lodi."

Marcos moved to turn on the light over the sorting station, but paused, snagging on Lizzie's information. The tips of his fingers hovered over the switch as he digested the information. "Lodi."

Lizzy nodded.

Marcos abandoned the idea of turning on the light and spun to face her. "That's nearly an hour away! Nothing good comes from Lodi." Who hired this guy? Might as well accept applications from Australia at this rate. Not to mention, in addition to that long hour drive which he was certain to get tired of after week two, there was that curvy road that snaked through about half the drive. No cell phone service to call if his car blew all four tires and he wasn't going to make it into work. The deer population was enough to cause humans to go extinct in that area, except when they ran out in front of the vehicles. Not that these parts got much snow, but any precipitation, whether frozen or liquid, over three inches was enough to keep you home because no one wanted to sail around a hairpin curve with three inches of rain on the road.

Lodi. Great. Marcos could already feel his anticipation deplete.

Lizzy huffed a small laugh and rolled her eyes before setting her gaze back on Marcos, trapping him in a stare that seemed to say, *oh, whatever!* She wasn't buying it. She, the light of the post office, the spring in everyone's step, the positive one outweighing everyone else's negativity and realism. "Well, you're from here, and people say that about you!"

Yeah, yeah, yeah. Marcos rolled his eyes, giving that *whatever* look right back to her. That word and look volleyed back and forth between them, and they hadn't even started their day. Shaking his head, he flipped on the light. "Well how old is he?"

"Eighteen."

Perfect.

Marcos spun around with determination. "Eighteen?" His frown deepened, his tone appalled. "He's just a baby!"

Lizzy's teasing look turned to admonishment. "Give him a little slack. He may be a good kid!"

Well, at least he had Lizzy to plead his case for him. If this were a courtroom and she was his attorney, he might do well. But Marcos's evidence consisted of the track record of "good kids" he'd seen in his lifetime. Sure, they might be good. But did they know how to count change? Carry on a conversation that wasn't typed through a screen? *Write* a letter, let alone send one? Shoot, the word *initiative* to them was little more than the sound you make when you sneeze!

"Eighteen," he muttered. "I'll be babysitting all day."

A dull *thump* sounded from outside. Lizzy's head whipped around to look toward the front before she threw a scathing look back at him. "Shhh, I think that's him that just pulled up."

She trotted to the other side of the counter and approached the window. She gazed out for a few seconds. Her voice bounced against the glass, echoing back at Marcos with more than a little warning. "Remember. If he quits like the last three, you won't have a vacation for a while!"

Marcos gulped back any retorts he might have said and finished it off with a sigh. "Okay." He held up a hand and busied himself with the little bit of sorting he had. So. The new guy was here. Probably ought to at least try to make him feel welcome. A vacation would be nice. Maybe a smile would do the trick? Marcos tried. His lips parted, showing off his teeth in a grin. *No, too creepy. Don't want him to think I'm a psychopath.* He kept his grin but closed his lips over his teeth. *No, too tight. He'll know I'm faking it.* He lessened the grin to just a small smile. *No, that won't work, either. Don't want him thinking I'm sizing him down. I am, but he doesn't need to know that.*

The door cracked open, just as Marcos found a more natural smile. It took thinking about a vacation to find it, but he succeeded.

Chapter 3

The door opened, and in strode Marcos's trainee for the day. Marcos braced himself as he turned around to lay eyes on the man.

Well, man was generous. It was more like *kid.* Was he even eighteen, Marcos wondered? Maybe he lied on his resume, because he looked more like fourteen. Tall and lanky, with unkempt blonde hair and hooded eyes. Not from age, but lack of sleep. Considering that it was a little after eight in the morning, that wasn't a good sign.

Marcos stood as Lizzy took over all the pleasantries. "Good morning!"

The kid – okay, James – nodded. "Morning," he said in a voice that was about as heartfelt as a gravedigger's.

Lizzy gestured to Marcos, keeping her tone light and cheerful, not befitting the mood. "This is Marcos, our carrier. He'll be training you on the route."

Be nice, Marcos reminded himself. *He might be a good kid.* "Good morning."

"Good morning," James said with a little more enthusiasm.

"Well." He was already late. Might as well waste no more time than necessary. "Come in the door over here. Its time to start." Marcos opened the side door that led to the back and James walked back like a lost puppy. Marcos already felt his muscles tense, a headache teasing him. How long before the shift was over?

As James passed, he remained oblivious to Lizzy raising both her eyebrows and rounding her eyes. It wasn't a look of warning, it was a look of *Calm down. Now.*

Whatever.

Marcos led James to the back, a room that was so familiar to him. While the walls blocked out the sun, the fluorescent lights did a fine job of lighting the room. "So, how did you like that training in Little Rock?" He kept his voice lighthearted, the same kind of charisma he was known for. He didn't show his hesitation over the new guy; he couldn't. This one had to work out.

Was it illegal to make bets with yourself? Marcos tried to remain positive, but another part of him was willing to bet his vacation time that this kid wasn't going to last more than a week at best. Maybe two, if he was lucky.

James shrugged slowly, not even putting effort into a shoulder plop. "A lot of boring, repetitive stuff. Some of it didn't even seem to be for mail delivery."

Well, at least he was good at making conversation. Marcos couldn't count the number of teens with whom he had interacted, where it was like pulling teeth to try to get them to say a sentence of more than three words or mumble. "Yeah, it's more about thinking. That, and telling you stuff so fast, just so they can say you were told."

He pushed through the doors into the casing area. What was probably foreign territory to James felt like home to Marcos, complete with the shelves of mail lining the back wall, carts and totes lying around, forming a nice workstation to sort the mail. A job that would likely be James' first test of endurance.

"They told you about DPS, didn't they?" Marcos asked.

James nodded. "Yes."

Yeah, Marcos had heard about it too. The Delivery Point Sequence, where a nice little machine sorted all the mail in the order in which it would be delivered. Marcos had only *heard* about it for various reasons. A slow, evil grin worked its way onto his face, ear to ear. He turned slowly to lock gazes with James. "Yeah, we don't have that here."

Lizzy came into the back room just in time to hear the latter bit of the conversation. She rolled her eyes, somewhat ruined by her playful smile as she shook her head.

James blinked for a moment before breathing out a laugh. "Oh, that's a good one!"

Oh. He thought Marcos was joking, did he? Lizzy and Marcos joined in his laughter. "Yeah. Sadly, it's true." Marcos stared, for the record.

The laughter stopped, not surprisingly. James didn't even try to hide the shock on his face. Marcos could almost guess what he was thinking. *Wait, what?*

"This is the only manual post office left." Marcos maintained his grin, as if this were the happiest news he'd ever dished out. He spread his hands and gestured around the casing area. "You're lucky."

This time, James's laughter was more forced as he scratched his head. "Yeah....right."

Lizzy course-corrected herself to walk right by Marcos and elbowed him in the ribs as she went by. "Remember," she muttered through pursed lips. "Vacation, vacation."

Oh, right. So why not blend a little sweetener into the bitter truth? Granted, the sweetener was artificial, but at least it wasn't bitter, either. "But it's not bad." Marcos hastened to follow up the negative with the positive. "I been doing it 16 years."

That was almost the amount of time James had been alive. It showed in the way the teenager raised his eyebrows. "That's a long time."

Marcos' grin turned mischievous. "Yep. That was your whole life."

A small crescent of a grin worked its way onto James's face. "Well. Not quite."

Well, enough standing around, Marcos thought. The mail wasn't going to deliver itself. Not that there was any mail, at the moment. Which was perfect, so he could use the empty time to show James around. He switched back into professional mode, maneuvering around the mailroom as he explained everything. "This is the sorting area. It starts at the top left," he gestured in the aforementioned direction. "And ends with the last box at the bottom right." His finger followed his directions. "We pull out of each cell from right to left." He eyed James to make sure he was listening. Eyes focused on where Marcos was pointing, James nodded. Marcos went on. "For each row, the first tray will be the last tray we deliver, and the last tray will be the first we deliver."

James's face clouded into a frown. He shifted uncomfortably, looking around at the, well, empty spaces Marcos was referring to. "Where's the mail?"

"Late as usual!" Lizzy called, annoyed from where she stood in the corner. "Ours comes from Shreveport. It is late regularly, and normally missing mail and packages."

"Oh." James nodded, probably just now realizing how his work was cut out for him. And it wasn't the start-on-the-dot job like he was expecting.

Lizzy trotted over with a stack of slips and showed them to James. "If someone asks you about anything missing, give them one of these slips." She ran her finger along the numerical portion of the slip. "It has the number here to the post office. Sometimes people are upset. If they are, just be nice and polite."

Marcos pressed another grin on his lips. James paled a bit as he took the slips, nodded, then awkwardly handed them back to Lizzy as if he didn't know what to do with them. Surely he wasn't expecting the people they worked with to be all sunshine and roses, right?

He...he did know that they did have to interact with people on occasion and not just mailbox to mailbox. Right?

Lizzy took the slips and sent a glance out the window into the front room. Her face clouded over with annoyance and dread. "Oh. Chill." She shot a glance at Marcos.

Chill? He hadn't even been doing anything for the past few seconds.

"It's time for you to be nice," Lizzy explained. "String Beans is coming."

Great. What a perfect way to start the new week. Marcos heaved a hefty sigh. "Oh heck. Why this early?"

"What's wrong?" James glanced up. The innocent confusion on his face was enough to make Marcos pity him.

"Don't look, James," Marcos said, quickly. "You won't be able to unsee it!"

Lizzy's face scrunched up as she admonished him. "Shhhh! Your voice carries!"

Marcos quietened down, but he wasn't able to stop himself from sending a side-glance out the window. James, too, let curiosity get the better of him. The door opened and Marcos braced himself for the encounter. It wasn't that the woman was the worst customer in the world. She was nice enough. It was just that they'd appreciate her coming around more if she'd used a bar of soap before entering the post office.

Lizzy walked up to the counter. From the tightening of her chest and the firm hold of her stomach, Marcos knew she was holding her breath. String Beans walked up to the counter. "Hello," she exchanged a greeting with Lizzy. "Can I get my mail? I don't know where my key is."

"Sure." Lizzy hurried to accommodate the woman. Speed was the goal; anytime String Beans was around, and it wasn't just for good, satisfactory customer service either. Marcos glanced at James, whose pale face had gained a certain green shade to it.

Lizzy returned with a stack of String Beans' mail. The woman took it and took way too long in shuffling out the door. Once the door had finally closed before her, Lizzy ducked under her workstation and aimed a can of Lysol at the lobby, shooting a spray of better-smelling substance into the air, setting the tiny particles free to do their invisible work of killing airborne germs.

As Marcos and James returned to their work, James looked at Marcos with a bewildered stare. "That woman needs a bra."

Marcos nodded. "Yep. And a bath."

James blinked. Maybe he was wondering where the balance of *be nice* met a statement like that. "That's kinda mean."

Lizzy returned to the casing area and shook her head at the same time Marcos did.

"Nope," Marcos confirmed. *Just brutally honest.* He went on to explain to the Lodi native how things were around here. "She has water, but for whatever reason, she won't use it. There are several people around here who are like that." He shook his head in bewilderment. "I've never understood it."

"If I don't spray the lobby," Lizzy piped up. "People complain that it stinks, and say it's my fault! They don't take into account people coming in and out of here." She kept working as she casually added the last part. "I had to remove the trash can out there because it was being used as a toilet."

Shock stretched James' eyes wider. He froze like a deer in the headlights as worry began to brew in his eyes. Heh, and Lizzy was the one telling Marcos to be nice and not run the guy off? This one was all on her. Marcos could almost read what James was thinking.

What have I gotten myself into?

***

What had he gotten himself into?

James took into account mentally what he'd encountered so far. Mail that was always late, meaning he had to wait around for who knew how long to start doing his job, so he couldn't get on the road faster, like he wanted. People who never used water and didn't know what a bra was, who came around the post office, stinking it up and blaming it on Lizzy. And trash cans, being used as toilets? In public? Out in the open for anyone to see?

The breakfast he'd crammed down his throat on the way over here slowly started to make its presence known in the form of nausea in his stomach. What kind of place was this?

Chapter 4

By the time the mail truck finally showed up, Marcos had shown James around enough to confidently say he'd done all he could do until the real job started. The kid wasn't bad so far. Green, yes, and naive, definitely, but at least he wasn't a belligerent, disrespectful youth who thought that he didn't need training because he'd already received it. But on the other side, Marcos knew he'd probably have to be the one to hold his hand for the first few days. The boy didn't have a lot of punctuality or initiative.

Vacation, vacation.

Lizzy wheeled the mail in and began the work of unloading it. "There's a lot of mail today," she commented.

Marcos and James stepped forward to help her. Marcos didn't mind the amount of mail they'd have to work through today. It was a great way to give the kid a crash course on what a day as a postman could look like. It took twice as long to sort it. Marcos could read the addresses in his sleep – in fact, he had a time or two, only to wake up and realize that a dog was not, in fact, chasing him. James, however, probably had no idea where any of these streets were.

"Go ahead and stand behind me to watch me sort this all in the case," Marcos instructed James.

James did as he was told with a single nod and stepped behind Macros. His eyes watched every movement Marcos made as he sorted the mail into the cases.

"We should be out of here in an hour and a half," Marcos quipped.

James's eyes grew wide. "Whoa."

"What?" Marcos tossed a bit of mail into its place in the case.

James shook his head slowly, eyes bolted onto the case. "I'll never learn 523 boxes! There is no way."

Wow, 523 boxes, I know, it's a lot. Definitely don't apply for a job in Little Rock. Or Hot Springs. Marcos wondered which comeback would be better.

Lizzy jumped in before he could say what was really on his mind. "Oh, you can do it! You passed the postal exams, you got this! It's much easier after a few days." Her voice danced with encouragement, showing even if she didn't believe it herself, she believed in him.

Marcos followed her example. Thinking twice, he did realize that five hundred boxes were a lot to learn for a newbie. "When we are driving the route, you will start memorizing names and boxes." He matched Lizzy's tone of lighthearted encouragement. "And in a few days, you will have it down, no problem." He paused for a moment, reaching to grab something from beneath the table. He straightened and handed a floppy folder to James. "Here is a list of every box, turn, road number and where a package should go if it don't fit in the box. At the end of the day, bring this back in the post office and leave it in this drawer."

Still bewildered, James took the folder and slowly opened it as if reading his own death warrant. "Thanks."

An hour and a half later, the sun had risen a bit more in the sky, beating down heat and humidity on the late Monday morning. Marcos, Lizzy, and James worked to load the SUV, and finally, the easy part of the job began. "See ya, Lizzy!" Marcos waved out his open window as Lizzy retreated back inside the nice air-conditioned post office that probably still smelled like Lysol.

James slid into the seat beside him. Marcos wondered if he thought this was some type of European vehicle, since he was in the driver's seat with no steering wheel. Marcos turned the car on. Warm AC not yet cooled by a running engine blasted him in the face, and his radio began playing a song from a Gospel station. James sent a scathing look down at the radio, and Marcos braced himself for a snarky remark.

"I don't want to listen to that," James stated.

Too bad, so sad. Oh, this was going to go so well. Rather than getting angry, Marcos grinned. "Well, it is my vehicle, and I will play what I want. I don't care if you like it or not." He put it in reverse, leaving no room for argument, and began to back out. "When you are driving your own vehicle, you can listen to what you want to." He put the vehicle in drive, adding as an afterthought, "But when you have a package or people are close, turn it down because no matter what it is, it will offend someone." Like the guy sitting next to him, for starters.

James gave it up. He sat back in his seat, pursing his lips, no doubt seething on the inside as Marcos took the familiar route to the first mailbox. Once there was nothing but them and the open road, Marcos took the reins of a conversation. Knowing he didn't have Lizzy there to remind him to be nice was quite relaxing. He could say what he wanted to say, all along chanting *vacation, vacation* in the back of his mind. He didn't mind the training, though he wasn't going to turn off his prankster spirit, either. "Now, just a heads up. People will grumble about you for a while till they get used to you. Also," he sent him a sideways glance. "You are at a disadvantage because you are a man."

He could imagine how his comment landed, leaving confusion in its wake across James' face. He pinched a frown into his lips and eyes and glances at Marcos. "How is that possible?"

Marcos went on to explain. "A young woman can look like she is about to cry, and it usually stops people from grumbling. She can act like she didn't understand, and most people will stop. It don't work for men, it just makes some angrier. Just be nice. It'll be okay. They will get over it in a day or two." He turned on his turn signal. "Well some will, anyway."

James nodded. "Okay."

Marcos turned up the first street and pulled up the first mailbox. He lowered the door, slipped the correct mail inside, and shut it. No incident. Five hundred twenty-two boxes left. Moving on.

Marcos pulled up to the next one, then the next. While watching the road and the mailboxes, he kept an eye on James. He noticed his Adam's apple bob up and down as he nervously watched the mailboxes, probably looking for the flag to be up and watching how Marcos did this.

They made it through ten boxes. Marcos was pleased with the progress. But by the eleventh box, a cute little barn-shaped thing tucked away in a driveway full of trees, an older woman shuffled her way to the mailbox, looked up the road, and waved to them.

Marcos pulled up to her mailbox, explaining to James. "Usually, there will be people who meet you and talk. Be nice," he repeated, again, wanting to drive the point home. "Talk a short bit and then go. We are the only people some will see or talk to for days on end." Even as he said the words, conviction made its way into his voice. Delivering mail was probably one of the most monotonous jobs he could've picked, but it was worth it to know that he could provide someone company, even if it was for five minutes in a day.

James acknowledged that he'd heard with a nod. Marcos pulled up to the mailbox. Mrs Henderson's excitement was obvious in the slight bounce to her step and the dance to her eyes, as if her best friends were pulling up, rather than just her mail carrier. "Good morning!"

"Well, good morning, how are you doing?" Marcos greeted her cheerily.

Mrs. Henderson peered into the car, eyes going straight for Marcos's sidekick. "Is this the new fellow?"

"Yes," Marcos nodded to the passenger seat occupant. "This is James."

James waved at her, but somehow seemed to lose his voice.

Mrs. Henderson leaned down to see him better. Marcos pressed his back against the seat and glanced over at James, hoping he remembered everything they had just talked about. *Be nice, and make conversation. You got this, James!*

"You remind me of my grandson." Mrs. Henderson beamed.

James's tight-lipped smile indicated that he wasn't entirely sure what to say. "I hope that's a good thing."

There you go, Marcos thought. Use a canned, scripted response if you have to, just make conversation.

"Oh, yes." Mrs. Henderson's eyes twinkled as the thought of her family brought her joy. She glanced at Marcos. "I hope you haven't been working him too hard, now?"

Marcos chuckled. "No, ma'am, just been riding around. He's been pretty good, so far." He glanced over at James, who smiled his thanks. When he glanced back at Mrs. Henderson, he adjusted the conversation a little bit. "So, what have you been up to?" He slipped the mail into the box, but wasn't ready to leave yet. Not when the woman's face lit up when someone stopped to talk to her.

"Oh, I've just been out in my garden. Speaking of which," she lifted her hands into sight and pushed two plump, ripe tomatoes through the window. "These are for you. Fresh from the garden."

"Well, thank you!" Marcos took the tomatoes and handed one to James.

"Yes, thank you," James called from his side. It took a tomato to break the ice as he found his voice again. "I love tomatoes." He bit into it, thoroughly enjoying the sweet taste of a garden-ripe tomato. "This is great!"

Mrs. Henderson's smile was radiant, as if complimenting her produce had made her day. "I'll try to leave you some in the box from time to time."

"Thank you!" James smiled around a mouthful.

Not wanting to get tomato juice all over the steering wheel or the mail, Marcos set his aside for the moment. "Well, I guess I'd better get on out of here and act like I'm doing something."

Mrs. Henderson laughed. "All right, you be careful, now! And, you." She pointed at James. "Don't let him work you too hard, now!"

James smiled. "Yes, ma'am."

Marcos pulled away from the mailbox with called goodbyes. James leaned around Marcos and took in the sight of Mrs. Henderson's garden as they passed, munching happily on his tomato. So far, it looked like he was enjoying his job. The garden was the sight to see, with rows of thick, brown soil, almost black, and luscious green tomato plants across from rows of other produce, perking up the garden. It could be enough to be a showroom garden, Marcos had often thought, with great vegetables and a bumper crop each year.

"Wow!" James exclaimed. "Man, that is a good-looking garden. The soil is so dark, it must be rich." No doubt he was excited about the prospect of receiving more tomatoes and maybe other vegetables in the future as a present waiting for him in the mailbox. Maybe some peppers, maybe some nice green onions, or carrots.

Marcos nodded, glad he was able to make conversation. Seemed like the visit with Mrs. Henderson had brought him out of his shell a little bit, since the tense moment over his Gospel music. "Yep. The sewer feeds it."

The tomato was halfway to James' mouth when his face suddenly paled. His eyes went wide. Stunned, he slowly turned his head to face Marcos head-on. "W-" He stuttered. "What do you mean?"

Marcos comfortably leaned back in his seat. "Well, a couple of years back, it started leaking there. Seeds sprouted and grew very well, so now she plants them there each year. It's close to her house."

Marcos was just making conversation, and no laugh curved his mouth to indicate that he was joking. He wasn't. And the moment James realized this was more obvious than if he'd said it. He looked down at his tomato. Back up at Marcos, then back down at his tomato again. "Please pull over."

Marcos glanced at him. "What?"

"Please, pull over!"

Marcos sawed the steering wheel, aligning the car with the shoulder. James threw the door open, leaned out, and emptied the contents of his stomach.

Marcos cleared his throat, patiently waiting until he was done. James leaned back into the car and closed the door behind him, wiping the sleeve of his shirt across his mouth. He no longer had the tomato in his hands, Marcos noticed. "That's just wrong."

Marcos wasted no time pulling back onto the road after checking for traffic. "She lives alone. It helps her stay afloat, along with her social security."

The fact that Mrs. Henderson's garden helped her stay afloat didn't seem to appease James' stomach much. He rubbed his forehead and groaned, practically leaning on the door as Marcos drove along.

After a few moments, Marcos figured the best thing for James and his woozy feeling was to get his mind off of sewer-fed gardens and back on his job. "There are about 84 miles of gravel road we go down each day. The county does not maintain them well." As if to back up his statement, one of his tires dropped into a nice pothole, jarring James to sit up straight with an "oof!" Marcos kept talking, as though it never happened. "And when we cross into Oklahoma for a few minutes, the scanner will say we are out of bounds each day. And, speaking of, the roads?" He slowed a bit, avoiding a flat tire as much as he could. "One day, the county was dumping chunks of rock in the road to fix it. It sucked; it was so bad the grader operator said, 'We need to call the judge and complain.'" Marcos shook his head once. "And he was right. It was nuts. In other parts of the county, they use great road material, and the roads are smooth, but none of the county people live up here."

James nodded along as he listened, occasionally reacting to one of the rocks in question when Marcos' tired hit it. "Yeah, I can tell." He must've found his voice after his little episode with the tomato. "Bet that's hard on vehicles."

"Can be." Marcos shrugged. "That's why we drive this one."

James might have been embarrassed by losing his breakfast in front of Marcos, because the chatty shell Mrs. Henderson had broken him out of returned along the dirt road. Marcos could care less about the shell, however, and continued to fill the route with commentary. When box 30 emerged into view, he couldn't help but point this one out. Some fellows along the route had very unique quirks, and this one was too good to miss. Tucked back in some trees, the bay window faced the mailbox where a familiar figure sat, looking out. "That fellow there," Marcos gave an imperceptible nod toward the window, "Won't come out for a package, but he sits in that window watching."

James wasn't as worried about being covert as Marcos, so he fully turned his head to face the bay window. "Really?"

Marcos eased up to the mailbox. "He'll watch as we leave, and you will see him walk out to check it." Marcos flipped the mailbox lid closed and pulled away. James's curious eyes peered in the passenger side mirror. Sure enough, the door to the house cracked, and the figure at the window became the middle-aged man walking up the driveway, his destination the mailbox. "That's crazy," James mumbled against the window, his eyes locked onto the mirror. "He just sits, waiting for his mail?"

Marcos went adrift with melancholy for a moment. "He has nothing else to look forward to, sadly." A fact that was true of most. What would it be like to live where the thing you looked forward to the most was receiving bills and magazines every day? An idea sparked in his mind, dissolving the somberness into something more lighthearted, that appealed to the prankster in him. "You want to see something funny?" His lip creased with mischief and a small sense of rebellion.

"Huh."

Enthusiastic. But a response, nonetheless. "Watch this." Marcos pressed the brake and threw his jeep in reverse. Eyes locked onto the rearview mirror, he eased the car backward. The man stopped, breaking his stride almost as hard as Marcos put the brakes on. The man pivoted and started for his door again. By the time Marcos had fully backed up to his mailbox, the man had retreated inside his house, sealing himself inside.

"What in the world?" James laughed, bewildered.

Marcos put the jeep back into drive. "He's a strange dude. He may even have me beat!"

James gave a hearty laugh at that one. Then, he paused, looking around, as if anticipating that the manager would spring up from the center console with pointed finger and furrowed brow. "I thought we weren't supposed to back up like that."

Marcos shrugged. "We aren't," he said, entirely unbothered. "I will have a flag on my driving today. Might even get a call, but wasn't it worth it? And it was a good lesson for you."

James' stoic face melted into something a little more pleasant, and Marcos quietly celebrated the victory. This was going to be a long day if the kid sat speechless in the seat next to him. It was too long a route for a one-sided conversation with another human being. "Glad you think so." James sat in his own silence for a few moments before he finally had to admit. "It was pretty worth it." He glanced back at the house, seeing the man hesitate at his door to make sure they were fully gone before starting up his driveway again.

"He is really a nice fellow." Marcos threw a look at the man in the rearview mirror. "But he doesn't like interacting with people. Now his sister, on the other hand, will talk your ear off. She comes to see him every so often."

James faced forward again, ready to knock out the next few boxes with a little bit better attitude. He traded sulk for conversation, for which Marcos was grateful. "Well, I probably couldn't get a word in edgewise, then."

Speaking of edges, Marcos thought.

No sooner had the words slipped from James' mouth than he turned on a one-lane dirt road. The road narrowed to the one-lane bridge that should be illegal, but wasn't. First off, who made a bridge out of wood anymore? Second, if you're going to make a one-lane bridge, at least have some sides or runners.

Well, it didn't have any of those. But it did have holes.

Marcos noticed James' discomfort as he squirmed in his seat. About halfway across the bridge, Marcos eased to a stop, pointing out the windshield at a massive hole they had to navigate around.

"See any fish down there?"

James shook his head rapidly, holding onto the handle on the roof. "No. I don't like this." His voice tight, James began to sweat.

Marcos chuckled a bit, working to straddle the hole as they rolled across it. "It's kinda cool, ain't it?"

"Mh-hmm." James continued to shake his head.

"Just don't get your tires in the holes. "

James' shallow breathing contributed tot he wooziness his in his eyes. "When will they fix it?"

"They did," Marcos assured him.

James turned slowly, as if any sudden movement would cause the vehicle to capsize. Marcos could practically read the words, *no, they didn't* in his eyes.

Safe to say, the bridge was better than it was. "It used to have boards missing and gaps between the boards. When the water is over it, don't cross. Because a previous carrier had their truck stall back there, and flooded."

"If there is water anywhere around that, I'm not crossing it!" James stated, firm with boundary. "That is nuts, that's not even safe!"

Marcos laughed as the jeep finally idled back onto the road, wide enough for his tires to stay between the lines. "I worry about your generation. This was a good bridge when I was growing up, and these roads back then? You could barely meet anyone; they were so narrow and swirly. Oh, and we didn't have cell phones or internet, and we survived."

James didn't take his eyes off Marcos. "You sound like my mom."

"Well, it's true." There was a reason Marcos sounded like James' mom, and everyone else in his generation.

Marcos angled the jeep onto Red Dog Road. If the house they'd left wasn't bad enough, this road was a real treat. "These people are funny." He nodded out the window to the road stretching ahead of him. "One of them dug a ditch across the road a while back to make the others mad."

"Really?" More comfortable now, James angled himself to face Marcos, leaning against the jeep's B-pillar.

Marcos nodded. "Yep. I called the county judge and told him that mail delivery has stopped on that stretch of road till the ditch is filled. They had someone out there a couple days later. You can still see a little dip where he dug. It's right there." Marcos pointed to an elongated pothole across the road. "It was about eight inches or so. The grader did," he held up his hand, wobbling it like a see-saw. "Okay, filling it."

The jeep hit the ditch, further driving his words home. *Okay, filling it* was rather generous, but at least it was drivable. "Oof! Obviously." James's lip creased. "He fits in good around here."

His last mumbled comment made Marcos laugh. "Well, the same things are happening around where you live, I guarantee it. Some people have nothing better to do than make other people as miserable as themselves. The one that dug the ditch drives like the devil, but has slow-down signs in front of his house." Marcos shook his head at the irony of it all. "And that's the way it works around here. I think they get paranoid because they drive too fast."

"Sounds about right." James agreed. "They want everyone else to live up to their way of life, but they want to be free to do what they want."

Marcos detected a hint of bitterness in James's tone, as if his words carried a double meaning. He didn't pursue it. He couldn't exactly deny it.

The next hundred boxes flew by like lightning. While making conversation with James about this house or that, his mind busied itself with the parcels destined for each mailbox. As he neared 159, he recollected that in addition to a handful of mail, a package small enough to fit inside the mailbox had also been included. Pulling up to the box, he spied the owner hovering on the porch, watching their every move like a schoolmaster. Marcos grabbed the small package and the handful of mail. Another thing he remembered about the package was that it looked like someone had kicked a field goal with it. The corners all crinkled, the middle was smashed, and a stamp reading *damaged* angled across the front. As if it wasn't obvious that the package was beyond repair, they had to stamp it just so you knew. It didn't look like a rectangle anymore, more like a mangled geometry experiment. Marcos wasn't going to stick around long enough to hear what the owner had to say. He stuffed the package inside the box, then zipped away, a cloud of dust rising up behind him to signal his hurried departure. James raised an eyebrow as he watched him. "What's the hurry?"

Marcos slowed as they neared the next mailbox. "He is going to be mad when he sees that package, and he was watching us."

James frowned. "We had nothing to do with it."

"Yeah, but it's hard to get that through their head. And we are the ones they see."He glanced over at James. "Okay, we're getting to where we're nearly halfway through the first half. Go ahead and start handing me the mail as we approach each box. That way, you can learn what addresses go where."

"Okay." James reached into the bin to do as he was told.

Marcos took the familiar route through the small town, only instead of roads with ditches plowed across them, a new challenge faced the would-be driver, sitting in the passenger seat. The town wasn't all paved roads and promises; some of the back roads were bad news for anyone not paying strict attention to the road and the angle of their tires. On one of the steeper routes, the road narrowed, loose gravel crunching under his tires, and the side of the jeep hovering precariously close to a cliff-like drop off. James sent a look out the window and stiffened. Forgetting the mail, he reached up and clung to the Oh-Crap bar. His eyes were glued to the window and the terrifying slope, worthy of the Rocky Mountains just outside his door.

Marcos slowed the car, caution overtaking speed. "How do you like that drop off over there?"

"Mm-mm." James obviously didn't want to look anymore. His head shook, indicating just how he liked it as he focused on something out of the windshield. "If a truck went off there, it's gone!"

"That is why you go slow up through here." Marcos chuckled a bit. "There is another spot we will run across, even steeper and deeper. Just be careful driving out here. There are very few people that drive this road and a lot of these other roads."

"I don't blame them," James confirmed, along with his pale face. Mercifully, after a few miles, the road widened again. When the route was finished, Marcos eased back onto the highway, hitting a mailbox just as James rummaged through the bin beside them. "We don't have any mail or package for this one."

"I know," Marcos replied. "But always check this box, whether they have mail or not. Be sure to look in this box for outgoing mail. They won't put the flag up, and they will complain when their mail doesn't get picked up."

James snorted a bit. *Like that's our problem,* Marcos could read the retort in his eyes.

Marcos pulled the lid down, examining the inside of the box. Confirming there was no mail, he pulled away. "I had to start recording when I have no mail for them, because if there is mail and the flag ain't up, we don't stop. That wasn't good enough, so we have to check it."

James' eyes drifted toward the dash. "I was wondering what that dash cam was for."

"Yep." Marcos nodded. "It can be a lifesaver, as well as these scanners." He held up the scanner in question. "The scanners typically gives us trouble, but the GPS says my speed and will show where the package is delivered, and if I'm sitting long, the post master will call to see if I'm okay. I have had a couple of people over the years who said their package didn't get there, and this technology showed they did." *Talk about accountability,* Marcos added, silently. He knew he'd always deliver packages, but without the scanners, he doubted some of the others on the route would. Maybe they'd spy something from Amazon Prime that they want for themselves, or maybe a card that was bulging too thick. "On this route, we get it done and done right without problems, so I typically don't get called. Others get called daily. Don't be one of those."

"I don't plan to be," James answered.

"Each day, do your best, even if someone tries to make it bad. You will see that the majority of the time, people are great, and you will figure out where to tread lightly as well." Marcos had 16 years to learn the town, and he was more than willing to pass along that information to James. He settled back into the seat to drive the longer stretch in quiet, thoughtful words. "As I have said, we are the only people that some of these people will see in a day or week. We should make that experience a good one, no matter what. We work for them. I believe God expects me to be nice, and help them if I can."

A storm brewed on James' face, surpassing the disgust he'd shown to Marcos' radio, earlier that morning. "I think we should be nice. But as for God, that's your opinion." He spat the words between tightly clenched lips.

God must be a sore subject with the kid, and Marcos knew better than to press it. Normally, he'd tease or make a comment, but he sensed this wasn't the time. They had the entire week to learn the route together. Marcos could wait to bring it up again until he knew the kid better. But until then, he backed down. "Okay," he conceded. Now wasn't the time. Maybe he'd try again tomorrow to find out where James was coming from.

Jem Johnson's box marked a little over the halfway point, and the day was flying by. Marcos pulled up to the mailbox, surveyed the surroundings as he always did. One could never be too careful on the mail route, no matter how small a town it was. His eyes went straight to two boys sitting on the porch. Both of them snickered as they watched. What were they snickering at?

If that wasn't about suspicious.

Since the mailbox was on James' side, he let James sort the mail and put it in the mailbox. He was expecting it when James opened the box, then immediately slammed it shut. "Go, go, go!"

"What's wrong?" Marcos didn't pull forward.

James snapped around to face Marcos. "It's a snake!"

Just as he expected. Any time two boys were laughing as they watched something, it usually boded ill. Usually had something to do with critters found in the wild. Snakes, frogs on their teachers' desks, you name it. "Stay here. Let me have a look."

Marcos got out, slowly taking his time as he walked around to James' side of the jeep. Taking his time, he opened the mailbox like a drawbridge, expecting something to come snapping out at him.

Fool me once, shame on you.

Really, James? He hadn't opened the box long enough to look.

Much to James' astonishment, Marcos reached in, grabbing the snake by the neck. He watched in frozen horror as Marcos returned to his seat as he plopped the supposed reptile through the window. James writhed and crammed himself against the door. "What are you doing…" His voice trailed off when he realized.

It was plastic.

Calmly, Marcos waved at the boys, acknowledging their prank. Shaking his head, his lips creased with a grin, he nodded to the mail. "Go ahead."

James released a sigh through his lips and shook his head. He picked the snake up, along with the mail, shoving it in the box just as Marcos got in. Anger lined his face as a shudder raked its way down his body.

"What?" Marcos laughed, leaving the mailbox behind. "They were just having a little fun."

"It's not funny!" James was beside himself. "Why would they do that?"

One for dramatics, was he? Cheery. "Relax." Marcos grinned, evilly. "They were just warming you up. Did you not ever have fun when you were younger?"

James glared above his folded arms. "I never did anything like that."

Marcos found that as easy to believe as saying algebra was fun. "Really?" He arched an eyebrow. "I mean, growing up, we were always fishing, hunting, or just some kind of harmless prank. One time, I packed my brother's cigarettes with black powder. I heard it was a blast." He laughed at his own joke.

James did not. He appeared to still be hung up on the two kids who'd hurt his pride. "Harmless?! My heart nearly stopped! I was sweating so hard, I'm soaked, now." The damp underarms and glistening hairline added truth to his tale. "And, I have to use the restroom."

Of course he did. He couldn't wait until they got to the corner store. Laughter bulged behind Marcos' lips. "Okay, hang on a second."

He navigated further out into the open. Once he was sure that no houses with cameras were around, he eased to the side of the road, then stopped. He put the car in park and waited expectantly.

James looked back at him with the same expectancy. "Why did you stop here?"

"You said you needed to use the restroom." Marcos waved his hand at James and the door. "Walk out there and take care of it. Watch for chiggers, snakes, and ticks." He gave the instructions in total nonchalance as if it were something one does all the time. The truth was, they did. It was James who probably never had to rough it in the wilderness in his life.

James was not amused, and it showed on his face. "I have to do the other," he admitted slowly, bitterness tainting his tone.

Man, that snake really scared him, didn't it? Marcos reached around into the back seat, feeling around the floorboard until the touch of fraying toilet paper met his touch. He grabbed it and brought it forward. "Here's some toilet paper."

James stared at it. He looked back out at the wilderness. Finally, the most definitive "No," spewed from his mouth.

"No?" Marcos added the *are you sure* in his tone.

"No!" James snapped back to see him. "I'll wait! Surely there has to be something else."

So much for a good first day. It had been, up until he got his feathers ruffled all over a snake. And a tomato, but that was different. Goodbye, vacation. "Yep. In about a half hour."

James stared at him, fully expecting him to bust out laughing. When he didn't, he huffed a sigh. Digging his fingers into the toilet paper with rage, he got out and trampled through the woods.

Marcos grabbed a magazine someone had returned last week and began reading. He glanced at the clock every so often.

Five minutes went by.

Marcos thumbed through the pages, reading all about overpriced fishing gear and what time of year to fish for each breed. Stuff he knew, but it was something to pass the time. He glanced at the clock.

Ten minutes.

How long could it take? Trying not to be antsy about getting back on the road, Marcos lowered the magazine, scanning the woods for any sign of life. *Did he get himself lost?* Great. How was he going to explain to the postmaster why he had to rough it in the wilderness, possibly battling off some sort of wild animal like a forest ranger because his young trainee's GPS didn't work in the field? Most importantly, how would he explain why?

Okay. Five more minutes. Marcos would give him five more minutes. He glanced back at his magazine. Read about the different types of trout.

Four and a half.

He scanned the rest of the article for any useful information, retaining none of it.

Fifteen minutes.

Marcos flipped the magazine closed and was just about to turn the car off when movement caught his eye. A lopsided teenage boy – his trainee – trudged out of the forest. Well, he was alive and not lost. That was good news at least.

"Whew," Marcos breathed out. He waited until James got back in the car, slamming the door closed, and tossed his half-gone roll of toilet paper in the back.

Dang.

"I done thought you were lost!" Marcos exclaimed, nervous laughter mixing with his statement.

James folded his arms and tucked his chin against his chest. His narrowed stare was nearly strong enough to burn a hole through the windshield. "No. I got caught."

Oh, that explained it. Marcos tried to breathe so that his laughter wouldn't come flying out.

"And had to explain myself." James didn't even move. His face inked red, and Marcos wasn't sure how much was embarrassment and how much was rage. "And when I told the man I was the new relief carrier, he laughed entirely too hard."

Marcos was tempted to do the same.

"I was not amused," James stated, for the record.

"Was it Bluebird?" Marcos asked.

James just nodded. "I think it was."

"Don't worry," Marcos quipped. "That story will be much bigger in the morning."

The last few words came out in wheezes of laughter, which faded as James shook his head. His jaw tightened and his eyes narrowed with further anger. Marcos swallowed his humor and said, reassuringly, "It's okay. It'll get easier."

That is, if he stuck around long enough to let it.

Finally, after what felt like an eternity, Marcos drove the final stretch back to the mailroom. "So," he pulled James out of his foul mood long enough to ask him a question. "What do ya think about it?"

Exhausted and worn out, James looked over at Marcos, sweat glistening on his brow. "Well, it's rough."

Rough. At least he picked that word instead of impossible. Marcos couldn't deny the word rough.

James snorted again, looking back out the windshield as if he'd just walked across half the US on some fantasy quest. "Man," his head shook side-to-side like a ghost hunter's. "That is a lot of boxes, and the roads are awful!"

Marcos cut him a grin, trying to keep the mood light. "You'll need some good all-terrain tires to be on the roads, but you will get used to it pretty quick."

James narrowed his eyes into a glare. "And the people."

Yes, yes, the people.

"Why are they so petty?"

"Well," Marcos shrugged. "They're partial to their mail, and for some of them, that is all they have to look forward to, even if it's junk mail."

A sorry look crossed James's eyes, too young to comprehend the aching loneliness some adults faced. "That is sad."

Another thing Marcos couldn't deny. One reason why being nice came naturally to him on the mail route was that even when someone was yelling their head off at him because their magazine jacket was ripped. Marcos was lucky to have a family that loved him. He couldn't say the same for everyone else. "That is just how it is most of the time. Most of the people around here are older, but many have kids or grandkids living with them. Normally, you will not see that many each day, but we were running late today, and they look at their clocks. So, don't expect that much interaction, especially in winter, unless it's a pretty day."

James nodded, relief dousing his face. Marcos pulled into the post office's parking lot and aligned his car with the curb. He killed the engine for the last time that day, ready to pick it up again tomorrow. He nodded between the seats. "Grab the outgoing mail and packages in that tote, and I'll grab the other trays and totes."

James nodded, doing what he was told with movements as slow as molasses. He stumbled out of the car, Marcos at his heels with the tote. Closing the door behind them in a quiet post office, Marcos nodded to the scanner in James' hand, glad he grabbed that, too. "Hang the scanner up on the third station. The other two don't work correctly."

James paused near the station, closing his eyes for a moment. "It feels good in here," he said as he allowed the AC to caress him and soothe away the sweat from the day.

"Yeah, it's hot outside and it's not even the hottest part of –" He stopped, already wondering if James would be back tomorrow. If he threw one more negative thing at him, probably not. "Yeah, it gets much easier."

James merely nodded.

Not wanting to sit in the awkward silence for more than necessary, Marcos quipped, "Well. I'll see ya in the morning!"

James nodded. "Okay."

Okay. That sounded so encouraging.

***

So, how was your first day?

After what felt like an endless shift, James curved his car around the windy road back to Lodi, dreading the question. It wasn't like it was horrible. Oh, no, not horrible at all. Just eating food that came ripe from the sewer system with who knows what else, getting scared half to death by a snake, fake or not, and getting caught mid-restroom run and having to explain why he was out there. On top of it all, a trainer who didn't seem to take any of that seriously. He didn't get it. And, he was one of *those* people. The kind that cram their faith down your throat. He'd brought up God once, and James had to stomach that Gospel music the whole time. No wonder he'd thrown up by the first ten boxes. He never wanted to hear the words *praise* or *hallelujah* again.

And a lot to learn. Like, so much to learn. 523 boxes. Could he do this?

He had to. He didn't necessarily love the idea of working, but he needed money. And delivering mail wasn't flipping hamburgers at some fast food joint, which at this point, was his other option.

James cranked up his metal music, letting the angry guitar drown out his rage. Maybe tomorrow would be better. Maybe he could fall asleep tonight and erase every nasty memory clinging to him from this first day on the job.

***

After the incident with the tomato and having a stranger in his car, Marcos wasn't about to put the car away without cleaning it first. The moment he went home, he hooked up the shop vac and let the roar of the vacuum fill his ears. The vacuum took care of the crumbs, dirt, and tiny pebbles lining the inside of the vehicle, little hitchhikers when he'd get out to deliver the mail. Once the roar of the vacuum died down, Marcos grabbed the hose and cranked the water on full volume, angling the spray to cleanse the dirt from the car. He shook his head. "What a day."

Chapter 5

The familiar screech of Marcos' alarm the next day was no less inviting than it had been the day before. In fact, maybe it was worse. At least when he was sleeping, he wasn't irritated by the constant reminder of his old job at the new day care, once known as the US Post Office.

Marcos decided to selfishly grab a few more minutes of rest for himself. He tossed to one side, staring at the wall. That didn't help. There was nothing to occupy his eyesight, so he let his thoughts drift back to James.

He tossed over to the other side, staring at his dresser, silently berating the clock for not stopping its downdown until he had to work.

"Oh, my." Marcos gave a sigh, slogged, and was heavy with grogginess. "Another day of babysitting," he rubbed his hands over his face. "Why, oh why?"

He forced himself out of bed with the effort of a man in chains and headed for the bathroom, trying to focus on his morning coffee routine. As soon as he slammed the door behind him, he heard his alarm going off.

No sense in trying to get some extra sleep.

He couldn't help but relate to the beans as he roasted them, feeling the heat and pressure of another day of being a kindergarten teacher. As he ground the beans to the same fine powder, he felt the same being done to his nerves at the mere thought of another day of this. For once, the coffee seemed to brew faster. As he poured it into his cup, he gave right of way to another groan as he headed out the door.

Maybe the car needed oil or an engine check. He could stop on the way to work. He turned the jeep on, seeing the dashboard lights come on, with nothing unusual.

Oh, well.

Marcos grumbled as he got into the car and headed toward his job at the prison transport.

I mean, mail carrier.

***

Beep, beep, beep.

No. Please no.

James' hand shot out of the covers, slamming down on the snooze button, then quickly burrowed under the warm covers again. Summertime was here, but the covers were too warm in the air-conditioned house to even think about getting up. His eyes were too heavy, his spirits too sagged. His energy was spent on an online early-morning video game showdown.

Beep, beep, beep!

Have mercy. Please. Five minutes took forever when it was four-fifty-five and he got off at five. But when it was counting down to get to work, five minutes became five milliseconds.

He slammed his snooze button again, avenging his broken slumber.

He descended back into a heavy REM cycle, dreaming about being surrounded by a bunch of beautiful blondes his age when...

Beep, beep, beep!

Saying something under his breath, James slammed his snooze button again. Did he really need to be up this early? Why had he set the alarm for six thirty? He didn't need to be to work until eight, and the drive was only forty minutes. Thirty if he sped, which he could, except through Langley.

His door flew open, and bright light flooded the room. James hissed like a vampire and flopped his arm over his eyes. "What in the..."

"James, you've got to get up." Mom approached the bed. James soon felt the covers whip back, and the cold air-conditioned air invaded his comfort. James groaned, but he didn't have time to recover before his mom started yanking his wrist. "You have to get up! You're going to be late for work."

Maybe he should quit. "I don't want to get caught in the woods again."

"What?"

Oh, that's right. He hadn't told her about that...incident. "Never mind. Fine, I'm up, I'm up," he snapped as he swung his legs over the side of the bed. He took a minute to try and force his eyes open.

"Get up."

"I'm up!" He sighed. Couldn't his mom give him just a second to recover? James straightened, shuffling into the bathroom and closing the door on his mother's endless *get-ups*. He took one look at himself in the mirror. Maybe that guy, Marcos, would see the heavy bags under his eyes, the red-rimmed slumber eyes, and have compassion on him.

James fluffed his hair with a brush, but that was all the effort the post office was getting today.

He threw on a shirt, not caring if it was wrinkled, or the same one he wore yesterday, and went out the door. He glanced at the clock, cringing that it was one minute late.

Oh, well.

***

Early, as usual. Marcos prided himself for not being late, and not even ever being right on time. His track record of sixteen years at the post office always showed him striding and clocking in long before his work was set to start for the day. Lizzy didn't have quite the track record he did, but it was close enough.

"Good morning!" Marcos greeted her with cheer.

"Good morning," she returned with her usual glimmer. She grinned, like an opossum eating thorns. "Soooo, how was yesterday?"

41

Yesterday. Marcos huffed a sigh as all the memories flooded him. If it wasn't the kid puking over a tomato – did he even know what compost was? It was him scowling at his radio or having the initiative of a potato. He was wondering if his *not-so-great* attitude showed on his face as much as it did in his person. "Well, I told you I would be babysitting."

Lizzy narrowed a stare at him, but before she could jump up and defend his cause, Marcos interrupted.

"That boy is citified. I don't see him making it. These people are going to chew him up and spit him out."

Lizzy's fit of giggles did nothing to soothe his nerves. "You know, you are acting *old!*"

Now, why did she have to go and emphasize the word *old?*

"You're acting grumpy, like my mom."

Wow, what a compliment. She wasn't out there to see him toss his cookies over a sewer-fed tomato, or expecting there to be a rest stop every five feet with Holden toilet handles. "Oh, now don't go there!" He had to chuckle in return. "I am nowhere near as grumpy as her." Old. He'd show her old. At least his back didn't snap, crackle, and pop every time he stood up. He had to add that. Had to defend his age, rather than show it. "And, by the way! She is a few years older." He pouted slightly.

Lizzy snickered. "Not much!"

"Yeah, yeah, whatever, now." Marcos laughed and seated himself near the counter, rather than jumping right into work. He was still waiting for his morning brew to take effect. He ran his hands over his face again and shook his head, looking over the tops of his fingertips. "It's hard to train these kids, and they seldom stay or stay for long."

Lizzy came around the side of the counter, a spring in her step as usual. "You have to loosen up and get one to stay so you can have a break. There is no one left around here to fill in for you. Everyone else's office is DPS. So, calm down."

Calm down. Marcos snorted and got to his feet. He took up a pile of magazines with addresses sorted about like a pile of jacks and began to sort through them.

Lizzy glanced out the window, then did a double-take. "Hey! He showed up, now. Be nice and happy."

The door creaked open. Marcos kept reading the magazine labels.

"Good morning, James!" Lizzy greeted with an extra dose of cheer for good measure.

Marcos glanced up. The sight of his trainee hit him like a roundhouse kick to the chest. Rumpled T-shirt, tousled hair, red-rimmed, puffy eyes, was it possible to roll out of bed and into work? Not even the forty-minute drive could wake him up?

Great.

"Good morning," he mumbled. A tombstone had more enthusiasm than he did.

Hoping that his over-the-top cheerful mood would annoy him as much as James' lack of effort annoyed Marcos, he quipped, "Good morning! Are you ready?"

Lizzy narrowed another glare at him. *Cut it out,* she said, nonverbally.

James slowly pushed his shoulders toward his ear lobes, just as he had yesterday. "I guess. But can we get done faster today?"

What? He...

He did not just say that.

Marcos stared at him, gritting his teeth to bite back the retorts that wanted to tumble from his mouth with the thunderous magnitude of the Niagara Falls. As if they had any control over how much mail to deliver. As if it were Marcos' fault, and not James. They would've been done on time if James hadn't let the sloths win the race against the mail sorting contest, or told Marcos to pull over a million times so he could either throw up his city boy stomach or go to the bathroom at inconvenient times.

Lizzy held her breath, looking between James and Marcos, bracing herself for a retort that would surely send James crying like a baby from the room. Marcos wondered if his eyes snapped as much as his mentality did. "I hope so."

Lizzy breathed a sigh of relief that made it to her eyes.

Marcos gave James a route order address list and pointed to the packages in the casing area. "Okay, first. Line the packages up while I sort the mail."

James studied the list, paling a bit. "Okay." He stepped up to the packages with the caution of a nervous dog. He was a few boxes in when Lizzy gave Marcos another warning glance. "Be nice. I think Leroy Jackson is coming in."

Great. String Beans yesterday, now this. Marcos chuckled a bit as the mailroom door came open. "I need popcorn for this." "*Shhhhhhhh!*" Lizzy hissed, then popped out into the front room.

Marcos forgot his annoyance with the kid and slanted a glance in his direction. "You gotta hear this." He jabbed a thumb over his shoulder and nodded backward.

"*Shhhhhhhh,*" Lizzy hissed a second time.

Marcos grinned, unable to control himself, and really wished he had some popcorn.

The bell dinged, letting everyone know there was a customer. Leroy, a linky fellow, strode over to his PO box. His slender, tall form bent to unlock the door to his mail. He took twice as long as anyone had, then shuffled his way to the window. The time it took him to get there was like the credits on a soap opera, you know was going to be good, you just had to wait for the show to start.

James continued to sort packages, ignoring the customer. Leroy walked up to the window.

"Morning," Lizzy greeted in her most cheerful tone.

Leroy stopped, doing a double-take at James as he cowered a bit. He pointed at James, asking in a dead serious tone, "Is he from the FBI?"

FBI? Him? Marcos' laughter bulged behind his lips. James just blinked, not sure how to take that.

"No," Lizzy shook her head, reassuringly. "He is the new relief carrier. This is James."

James waved politely.

Leroy angled his head to the side, eyeing James with suspicion. "I don't know. You gotta get that camera out of my box."

It was Lizzy's turn to blink. "What camera? There isn't one there."

"Yes, there is."

Flabbergasted, Marcos perked up. Was it really James who'd said that? James, who didn't know how to survive in the wilderness, let alone on the road, knew something that neither Marcos nor Lizzy did? James, who knew how to put mail in the box, then close the lid, and that was it?

Leroy's suspicion narrowed his eyes, Lizzy blinked, and James straightened, facing him. " There is, in the back. I saw it. It its small and round."

"What?" Lizzy came around the corner, Marcos at her heels. He had to see for himself. Lizzy approached Leroy's PO box and unlocked it, swinging it open. Her lips pursed, and her cheeks bulged a bit. "No, sir. That is a rivet."

James flushed bright red. Marcos should've known better than to think the kid had actually been observant enough to catch something.

Leroy nodded with all the seriousness one could get. "They are using it to control my TV."

Now was a good time for that coveted popcorn.

"Really?" Lizzy feigned interest, but disbelief hung in her tone.

Leroy nodded, up, down, up, down.

"Well," Lizzy cleared her throat, a last-ditch effort to control her laughter. "I'll look it over and see if I can disconnect it for you or put some tape over it."

"Thanks. I appreciate it." Throwing one more suspicious glance at James, Leroy shuffled to the door. The air was thick with lighthearted tension until the door closed behind the town's resident conspiracy theorist.

As soon as he was gone, Lizzy pointed her finger at Marcos and shook her head, eyes dancing with suppressed laughter.

Marcos chuckled, shaking his head. He raised his eyebrows and nodded his head out the door as he looked at James. "I told you to listen."

James didn't even blink, just stared at Marcos with an astonished, wide-eyed wonder. "He isn't on the route, right?"

"No, he's not," Marcos assured him.

Lizzy returned with a roll of black tape. "Come on, now, be nice." She yanked some tape off the roll and reached inside the box to cover the "camera" within.

Marcos laughed as he returned to sorting the mail. Distracted, James returned to his sorting. As they did, Marcos pondered what the day would bring. He wasn't about to let James sit around and be lazy this time. What better time to start him behind the wheel? He'd give it a few boxes in, then surprise James by switching places with him. Out there, where he couldn't get back to his car and speed away, thus never seen again. But that was for later.

Surprisingly, they finished sorting about the same time. James stuffed each package into their designated tote. Once he was finished, Marcos nodded to him. "Can I have the package list?"

James blinked. "What list is that?"

Today was not starting out well. How did he...Marcos blinked his disbelief. "The...the one that has the order of the packages."

James looked down, around the area. "Uh.... I didn't see one."

Marcos breathed in very, very slowly. "You did write the packages' addresses down, right?"

The time it took James to pause before he answered had the dread of a death sentence in court. Drumbeats of doom, seconds of disaster, draining all hope for a good day. "Um." Another pause. "No."

Marcos breathed again. *Vacation. Vacation. Vacation.* He imagined himself lounging on some beach in the Caribbean...

Yeah, like that would ever happen.

"I did put them in order, though!" James added, as if it somehow made things better.

Marcos needed one more breath to get through his next sentence. "You will have to look up the scan packages on the scanner. Not all will be there, so you will have to look at the packages closely and let me know which ones are on top of each layer."

James stared. "Okay."

It was everything Marcos could do not to show his disgust. He turned his face away and picked up his tote of mail. "Come on, let's head out. Grab the package tote." Because obviously, he had to tell James to do every single thing, or else, it wouldn't get done.

So much for the hope of getting done on time.

"That will be easy," James quipped, cheering up his voice to avoid conflict.

Marcos didn't grin. He knew if he said anything, it would come out bark and bite. They loaded the packages, then took their designated spots. Marcos wasn't ready to let James have the wheel just yet. He didn't want to wind up in New Orleans, so he'd wait until James woke up a bit.

He turned on the car, and the Gospel music took over the radio. Marcos wished he could crank it up louder. James's familiar scowl returned, and his lips parted with protest. The protest soon died. Maybe he knew he'd messed up and decided not to pursue it.

Good.

Marcos put the car in drive and started the day.

Marcos let his disgust and discouragement die after about ten boxes in. When they reached a pullover spot, he swerved the car onto the side of the road and grinned at James. "Ready to get behind the wheel?"

James eyed the driver's seat as if it were the plastic snake from yesterday. Looked back up at Marcos. "I don't know where I'm going."

"That's why I'll be in the passenger seat, guiding you! Plus, you have that folder I told you about yesterday," Marcos explained cheerfully. Just...Just...no package list. He was still salty about that.

Without waiting for James to come up with another lame and lousy excuse, he opened his door and stepped out. Standing there all tall and proud in his cowboy boots, Marcos waited a few extra seconds for James' door to pop open. Reluctantly, James shuffled around to the driver's seat of the jeep.

James didn't start to wake up until about three or so mailboxes in. He delivered the mail without difficulty until they came to a longer driveway. One that Marcos knew well. James pulled up to the Robertson's box. Just as he did, a glass-eyed dog tore up the driveway toward them. Snarls and barks rose over the roar of the engine before James even pulled the jeep to a stop. The dog rushed at the car, continuing to snarl as if they were the biggest threat to the home. The light blue eyes were too gentle for the ferocious nature of the canine. By the time the jeep stopped, the dog continued to bark, but crouched down to the ground, as if ready to pounce, and his rapid barks increased.

James eyed the dog. "What is that dog's deal?"

Marcos shook his head. "This is its daily routine. It's not mean; it will stop when you go a few feet."

James kept his eyes on the dog for a few more seconds. When he'd seemed to have enough, he reached down into the tote and withdrew the correct mail. He checked the addresses, something Marcos silently commended him for, but wished he'd do it faster.

Marcos wasn't sure if he'd talked about this house on the route yesterday, so he covered for it, today. "Leave the lid down on that box, but look in it for outgoing mail because they don't typically put the flag up. They get mail every day and just expect we will look."

James nodded, reaching for the open mailbox.

"And remember: don't close the lid."

Confusion darkened James' face. "I thought we are supposed to close the lid. That is what we were told."

Marcos nodded. "Yeah, that's Little Rock. If you close that lid," he pointed to the Robertson's mailbox. "They will call the postmaster in the morning, throwing a fit. And if you keep it up, they will start sending complaints. Reality and making the postal customer happy is our job."

James lowered an eyebrow. "Reality?"

"Yeah." Marcos blinked, cutely. "You know, when you say one thing, but mean another?"

"Oh. Right. You tell them it's not a big deal, when it is?"

"Exactly."

Reluctantly, James shuffled the mail into the box. Marcos could tell that it was everything he could do to keep himself from closing the lid, even out of habit, alone.

Marcos rested his arm on the open window, enjoying being the passenger prince for the day. "When it comes down to it," he said. "The customer is usually right even when they are wrong. People are funny about their mail. See that letter there that says 'or current resident?'"

Letting the engine idle, James picked up the letter that Marcos referred to. The addressee wasn't addressed to a name, but a *current resident.* "Yeah?"

"A number of people will put them back in the box written on it, 'this is not ours.' They will tear them up throw the pieces in the box or on the ground. You will also notice that wealthy people have mailboxes, and people who want others to think they are wealthy have P.O. boxes." He chuckled and shook his head. "It's very strange."

"Yeah, no kidding it is." With that, James tossed the envelope back in the tote and pulled away. Marcos continued his coaching over the roar of the wind in the open window. "Don't worry about what people have, or get. Or what they do. Just do the job and be nice, and it will work out. The majority of people here are good people, but can get sideways about their mail."

James nodded. Marcos wondered if he was still listening or if he had tuned him out, as it was the same information that they'd been talking about. He could almost read his thoughts. *Yeah, yeah, you said it before. Be nice, be courteous. Most people are nice, but some are not. I get it.*

Marcos returned his attention to the road. "I know I sound like a broken record. But that is what you need to remember."

James paused for a moment, maybe even thinking back on Marcos' words. Maybe he realized he'd been copping an attitude this whole time and wanted to make up for it, without apologizing. He laughed. Marcos would take it if that's all he could get. "My mom writes on those, and mail that goes to a different address."

Marcos matched his humor, letting an easy smile splay his lips. So James wasn't completely ignoring him and was trying to make friendly conversation as they drove.

"She says her mailman should know better." James went on.

"Really?" Marcos arched an eyebrow.

James nodded, a bit sheepishly, seeing as how he was talking to an actual mailman. "Yeah."

"So, she is a scribbler." Marcos breathed a laugh. "That's perfect."

James frowned in confusion again and tilted his head. "What?"

"We call those people scribblers," Marcos explained. "Because they could just put the mail back in the box with the flag up, but, obviously, they are perfect."

James hesitated for a moment. "Oh," he said while forcing a laugh between his teeth. Whether he was offended or just unsure of what to say, Marcos wasn't sure.

"When you have done this for a few months, you will have a different view," Marcos assured him. "You will see how dumb some people act. Especially people that should be smart, and to them, it may not be dumb. And some watch others do it." He laughed and shrugged, making a joke. "Must be something in the water."

They had nearly gotten through twenty boxes without event. It felt wrong. Something always happened before the twentieth box in. When box 17 came into view, Marcos wondered if James was having a day of beginner's luck.

He'd be wrong.

Marcos tensed, praying that James wouldn't wipe out the side view mirror on the mailbox as he pulled too close to it. The mirror barely grazed the mailbox, and Marcos decided not to chide him unless he did it more than once, consistently. He couldn't micromanage everything, or his vacation would go back to being a daydream.

James grabbed the correct addresses and opened the mailbox. Before he could slide the mail in, an angry buzzing sound filled the air. A tiny insect shot out from the mailbox, straight into the open window of the car. The wasp zipped past James' head, angrily.

"Ahhhh!" James leaned back.

Marcos looked over at the wasp, and his eyes widened. *Not today, Satan.* He plucked his door handle, jumping out of the jeep, leaving the door open in hopes that the wasp would just fly straight through and out the other side.

He did not. In fact, he flew back inside the vehicle to harass James. Heaving in panicked breaths and huffing out the same cries, James swatted at the wasp from where he sat, too close to the mailboxes to jump out as Marcos did. He swatted at the wasp with the mail, nearly hitting its body. The wasp buzzed back across his nose and as a result, the entire jeep bounced back and forth, evidence to any onlookers of a battle between tiny wasp and human.

Marcos calmly waited outside the vehicle as James kept up his act of shouting and swatting at the flying insect. The wasp ricocheted inside the jeep for a little bit before zooming low across the ceiling and buzzing out the other side. Marcos slid back into the seat, closing his door against the uninvited intruder and rolling up his window, just in case. "You seem a little scared of wasps." He glanced over, doing a double-take. A little scared might be an understatement. James's eyes were still wide. His chest heaved with rescue breaths pumping from his own lungs. Sweat glistened underneath his hairline and on his face.

"Well, you got out, didn't you?" James defended. "I couldn't! The mailbox was blocking my escape."

Marcos couldn't help himself but laugh a little. "If you stay still and turn the A/C up, they will leave."

The exact opposite of what James had done. He'd lost all composure and just barely began to regain it by the time he shoved the mail in the wasp's home, the mailbox, and moved the car back into drive.

Memories of prior trainees flooded Marcos, and he laughed again. "I was training this chick once, and there was a box that had this flap that would pop up when the box was opened so they could tell if they had mail."

James frowned as he tried to envision the mailbox, but nodded. "Uh-huh?"

"She opened that box, and a wad of mahogany wasps flew out and got us both."

James cringed. "Ouch!" Those deadly beasts, the wasps bearing the same color as their name, were known in the south to be some of the most vicious jerks around, who stung for no reason and could take over an entire area like cartel. Everyone also knew that you didn't want to get stung by one of them. If you didn't puff up twice your size, you'd wish they'd have just knocked you unconscious rather than stinging you and leaving you to live with the burn.

"Yeah." Marcos held up his arm. "Rotted a couple holes in my arm the size of a pencil. She came back – I think it was a Monday – a few days later. The wasp in the mailbox had been killed by then, and I told her that. When she opened that lid, the flag swung up, and I went," Marcos threw his hands in the air. "*Bzzizzzi!*" He hissed and buzzed his best imitation of a wasp between his teeth. It got a chuckle from James. "She nearly jumped out of the car."

"That's mean!" James shook his head as he chuckled.

"Then, she realized it was me. Came back in and whooped me." Marcos remembered the girl launching herself back in the vehicle, unleashing everything she had on him, landing hard smacks along his arm where his wasp sting was still healing, maybe a slap on his shoulder to go with it. "I was laughing so hard, I never felt anything. She didn't say anything the rest of the day."

"I bet she didn't!" James seemed quite entertained by Marcos's story. "Did she stick around after that?"

"For a while." Marcos chuckled. "A few days later, she could see some humor in it but not much."

James' laughter simmered for a bit longer. "That's great."

"You will see a lot of wasps doing this," Marcos nodded his head back to the mailbox they'd just come from. "And I won't say you will get used to them. But if you'll use the AC, it will get them out."

"Noted." James reached down to the dashboard and cranked the AC up as high as it would go.

"And another thing?" Marcos warned. "Never put your hand blindly in any box."

"You mean, without looking first?"

Marcos nodded. "The wasp was a perfect example. We find scorpions, wasps, spiders, all kinds of things in there."

James' Adam's Apple lifted, then fell as he swallowed. "Like that snake, yesterday."

"Exactly that. Sometimes kids will put things in a box, so if you see a rock or something, just leave it." Marcos drummed his fingers on the side of the door. "Oh, and the occasional real snake," he added as an afterthought.

James nearly brake-checked them through the windshield. "Real snakes?!"

Marcos chuckled against the seatbelt that locked him to his seat. Once James had the car moving again, he pulled it away from his neck. "Some of these kids keep us on our toes. A snake is ready to get out of the box when its hot. Some of these kids are little devils!"

James breathed a breathy laugh. "Yeah, I'd say so." The angry look in his eye was reminiscent of what had happened yesterday. He still had not forgiven those kids by the look of it.

"No," Marcos held up a finger. "I did not ever do that kind of stuff as a kid. What I *am* saying," he couldn't deny the grin smearing across his face, nor the laughs that overtook him. "Is that you still *are* one."

James glared, huffing a sigh. Sighs and eye rolls seemed to be his preferred method of communication, but that was fine. Marcos' was humor, so it worked out accordingly. "Very funny," James said, dryly. "But, no. I wasn't mean. Besides." He shrugged. "We had phones and video games while you had rocks and sticks." He side-eyed Marcos, an evil grin spreading across his lips.

Marcos' jaw dropped. He shook his head, laughing, despite himself. "Hey! I'm not that old."

James's lack of comment was all the commentary the young sprite needed as he turned back to the road.

After a few minutes of no wasps and no events, James rolled up to a pedestal of four boxes. He'd seen it yesterday, but his eyes still widened with uncertainty. Marcos didn't expect him to remember everything from his first day of training. Especially since by now, he'd still been recovering from eating a sewer-fed tomato and an adventure in the woods neither of them expected. Marcos leaned around him, pointing out each house for each box. When he pointed to one specific blue one, he smiled. "That house right there? My second-grade teacher lives there."

"Oh, yeah?" James leaned down to see the house settled at the tip of Marcos's point.

"Yeah. She's real nice. You don't see her much, but she is friendly when you do. Some of her neighbors are not as good. That one over there," Marcos drifted his point to a house precariously lumped down the hill. "Is a preacher-slash-elder and doesn't like her."

James frowned, looking back at Marcos. "Really?"

Marcos nodded. "It kinda knocks out that *love your neighbor as yourself* teaching."

A scowl darkened James' face. His body stiffened, as if ready to attack the idea that a Bible verse was in the same car as Marcos's Gospel music. What was next, praying over meals? "Well, people have different opinions, I'm sure." His tone was clipped.

"Yep." Marcos laughed. A semi-evil grin spread across his lips. "But mine are correct."

James rolled his eyes, topping it off with a huffed sigh. Marcos laughed as he rolled away from the mailboxes.

As James idled up to Box 19, Marcos eyed the driveway with suspicion. They'd gotten through yesterday, unscathed, but it looked like today was going to be another test for James, whether he truly wanted the job or not. The test's name was Mrs. Reynolds, and there was no multiple-choice answer with her. The middle-aged woman strutted up the driveway, flopping a wave in their direction.

Marcos returned her wave and a smile. Through gritted teeth, he told James, "Stay alert. She is a cougar."

James stiffened. "Okay." Marcos was pretty sure he heard James utter *great* under his breath. He rolled the window down to deliver the mail.

"Hi, there." Mrs. Reynolds leaned in to peer into the window.

James and Marcos both echoed "Hi" at the same time.

"Well, who's this young fellow?" Mrs. Reynolds aimed a flirty smile at James.

"This is my relief." Marcos introduced James, who cautiously nodded his head. Every muscle in James' stiffened posture screamed that he wanted to floor that accelerator and speed on out of here.

Mrs. Reynolds' lips parted in a pleased smile. "Hi, James. I'm Mrs. Reynolds. And can I just say, you're one handsome young man. I bet you're beating the girls off with a stick."

If this had been said by another eighteen-year-old, James may have swelled with joy. From a middle-aged woman, however, he fought to hide his cringe. "Thank you, ma'am."

"You are welcome to stop by and visit any time," Mrs. Reynolds was never very good at reading the room – or the mail delivery vehicle – and patted the doorframe near the open window. "I am home most of the time."

If that wasn't creepy.

"If you need a bathroom or a snack, you let me know."

Marcos held his breath for what James might reply to that. Something snarky, something with as much vitriol as he had for Marcos' Gospel music? James surprised him by forcing a polite smile. "Thank you. That's so nice of you."

Way to go, James. Marcos could've applauded him in that moment.

"I'd better get back to delivering the mail, but it was nice to talk to you," James continued to surprise him with polite evasion.

"You, too, honey." Mrs. Reynolds patted the window. "You look out for him, now, y'hear?" She aimed at Marcos.

"Oh, I will," Marcos assured her.

James pulled the car away from the mailbox, side-eying Marcos. Marcos was almost certain he saw his lip curl in disgust along with it. "She is old enough to be my grandma!"

Marcos gave a hearty laugh. "Hey, she said you are handsome."

Another scowl overtook James' face, and he sent the same scathing look toward Marcos. The look didn't intimidate Marcos as much as it humored him. "She is not quite as old as she looks. She is only, like, 42."

James blinked, returning his gaze to the road. "I thought she was a lot older."

"She dolls up good when she wants, and she is nice." Marcos granted her that. She had good manners. Maybe too good, but better to have too good manners than none at all, like some postal customers. His face softened as he recalled Mrs. Reynolds' story as easily as recounting the many tales he'd heard as a postal deliverer. "But she grew up rough. Most of her life was very hard. Occasionally, she goes to church. She seems to do better then."

"Oh." James sensed the heaviness in the conversation – that there were more layers to this cougar than the surface growl and fell silent.

James only had to check with Marcos for directions once in a while. Marcos happily provided them, as he didn't want James driving with one eye on the map and the other on the road. Twenty boxes soon turned into twenty-five. Being a passenger gave Marcos time to think, to reflect on the first few times he'd driven this route, when he'd been in James' position. He'd learned the route quickly, but also picked up a few life lessons along the way. Being a first responder had brought him into many people's lives on their worst days, leaving him with things he wished he could forget. Being a postman had brought him into their lives in a different way. Not necessarily on the worst day, but it gave him a peek into their lives. Some of those peers, like his memories, he wished he could forget as well.

This one wasn't bad, though. James slowed upon approaching the twenty-sixth box, as Marcos was overtaken with a host of quiet laughter. "When I first started, there was a middle-aged woman living here." He nodded to the house attached to Box 26. "She was a fitness fanatic, on the verge of becoming a bodybuilder."

"Really?" James angled the car into the shoulder, reaching to open the mailbox.

Marcos nodded. "Yeah. Not a chick you would want mad at you. I'm sure she could have opened a can of Whoop-Tail on you."

James breathed a laugh, stuffing her mail inside the box. She had quite a thick mess of letters today, but James placed them in her mailbox without bending any of them. The kid did seem to know how to do his job, and it showed in the carefulness he used so as not to bend or tear the envelopes."

"I had a package for her one cold morning." Marcos went on, cringing at the memory. "So I honked, scanned the package, you know the drill."

James nodded, closing the mailbox lid.

"Before I could get out, this woman came running out of the house to the truck in a 2-piece bikini." He looked up in the yard and could still see the barely-clad woman rushing out at him. The same shock and embarrassment flushed him on a more minuscule level as he recounted the tale. James' eyes went wide with the same shock. "Now, that was in the dead of winter. There was a heavy frost out."

"She was wearing a bikini in the dead of winter?" James exclaimed.

"She was. Some people around here!" Marcos chuckled. "She was very nice about it."

James pulled away from the mailbox rapidly, as if a two-piece bikini-clad woman were after him. He left with enough speed to make sure that wouldn't happen. "That's crazy!"

"She was tough," Marcos spoke through a series of chuckles. "I don't know what was in that package, but she wanted it right then."

"I don't think I really want to know," James admitted. "To come out of her own house in a two-piece bikini." He paused. A blush crept up onto his cheeks. "That... happens a lot?" His voice tightened, as if he were asking a question he didn't want to know the answer to. At least, not if the answer was anything but *no*.

"It can." Marcos remembered his earlier thoughts about sugar-coating the truth. "But it isn't as common as the big cities might get." He settled back, staring out the windshield. "With that, and other situations, you have to be polite, like you did with Mrs. Reynolds. Sometimes that is hard." His eyebrows rose, emphasizing his point. "But you have to. Sometimes you have to find an excuse to get on down the road. The scanners we have?" He nodded to the scanner taking up space in the console. "Both of them are GPS real-time, and they send signals back. The local offices can watch where we are, how fast we drive, how long we are sitting, and even an accident. I have been called before because I sat too long when someone was talking to me."

James threw a glance down at the scanner as if it were the lifeline he didn't know he had. "Do we get in trouble?"

"Well, they want us to keep moving as much as possible. You take fifteen minutes per house, times that by the five-hundred-plus boxes you have to do, and it adds up."

"Right." James' tone indicated that he didn't plan to stay for longer than he had to at any of the houses. Marcos wondered if he would give Mrs. Henderson or people like her the extra second or two to bring a friend into her day, to watch her face light up as he interacted with her. Mrs. Henderson was one of the sweet ones. Yet Marcos thought twice about sending James out to interact with someone like Mrs. Reynolds, or Two-Piece from Box 26. "A lot of the women are home when we come by. And some will wear nearly nothing."

The blush returned to James' face, but Marcos wasn't sure if it was the thought or the fact that he was trying not to look horrified and doing so meant not breathing.

"You just have to ignore it. I don't think most mean anything by it, or think about it, but some do. I've heard service workers like a/c repairmen or others talk about it, as well. Some may not get enough attention by their husband or don't have one."

"Like, how old?" James asked, with hesitancy lacing his tone. He fought off a cringe, ineffectively as he braced himself for Marcos' answer.

Marcos shrugged. "18 to 80, blind, cripple, or crazy."

You must be nuts. James shot the question through the slits of his eyes and the slight lowering of his jaw out the side of his face at Marcos. Marcos returned it with a smile. *It's true,* he nonverbally confirmed with a few nods of his head. He knew James would wish for a blindfold some days and a memory eraser for others.

James didn't seem to appreciate the answer like that. He rolled his eyes, settling them back on the road and the next mailbox when his eye-roll was complete. Marcos chuckled and pointed to the scanner. "The scanner is your excuse. Just tell them the post master or manager will call if you sit too long."

"Good to know." James exhaled a breath.

***

Getting flirted with by some old lady was bad enough. But...the thought of pulling up to a house with someone in their birthday suit or barely above it didn't thrill James at all. In fact, he'd rather eat another sewer-fed tomato than see some of these older women in their bikinis. Surely Marcos was exaggerating, right?

Surely.

Right?

Chapter 6

Even after thirty boxes, James wasn't doing half bad. Not professional, yet, though. Marcos could see it in the awkward way he responded to Marcos's instructions, such as a nod, a "yep," or a "no way!" when Marcos mentioned something that shocked him. But he'd managed to pull out some banter from that youthful mind of his, and he hadn't delivered one envelope wrong so far. He also nearly hit only a couple of mailboxes, which was less than what Marcos expected. And no damage to the vehicle so far. Always a plus.

See? What could go wrong? Yesterday was just one disaster piled on top of another for the kid, but today boded well for a better series of events. Marcos mentally counted off each mailbox in his head. *Thirty...thirty-one... thirty-two...*

Ah, yes, thirty-two. Another host of memories was hidden among the vegetables and flowers surrounding the house in a garden hedge. "I changed the tire for the elderly couple who live at the last box. They are very different and don't deal well with people. I'm not sure they even like me, but I wasn't going to leave them there on that narrow road."

"That's sweet of you." James aligned the jeep with the box.

Marcos hadn't done it to be sweet. He never wanted to leave anyone in need behind. He knew what that was like, and if he could help it, he didn't want anyone around him to ever feel the same way. "Being nice to people goes a long way. If you talk to him, he is loud. I don't think he has bad hearing; he is just loud."

James's gaze drifted up from the sorted mail between him and Marcos. "Oh? Is he louder than you?"

Ouch. Marcos let the comment land with a second or two of silence while he took the blow. This kid had a wit sharper than the letter openers in the mailroom. Marcos was too busy being impressed to take offense. That and, well. He couldn't exactly deny it. A grin of approval spread across his lips. "Everyone says I'm loud, but he has me beat. A lot of people around here are kin by blood or marriage or both, it is Arkansas."

The word *both* hit James, causing a scowl to wrinkle his face. "That's nasty!"

"It's still true." Marcos nodded his agreement. "Around here, word travels. Good words are slower than bad words. Some are close kin, too."

James laughed, stuffing the mail inside the box, and Marcos joined him in that laughter. "Man, that just isn't right."

"It's not." Marcos checked for traffic at the same time James did. This was the last house before timberland, as he'd come to know it. James seemed to have been barely paying attention through here, yesterday, and within reason. There wasn't anything to pay attention to. The road flattened out into an area where timber grew. Trees, some stripped of their leaves, poked above the ground like skeletons, reaching for the sky with bare branches, laced with bark. The air smelled of pine needles and evergreen. As James drove through, Marcos nodded out the window. "Keep an eye out when you come through here, because these trees die, then fall across the road."

James opened his eyes wider as if that would help him see better and gripped the steering wheel. "Okay."

"I had one fall right in front of me a while back." Why not scare the kid with a good true story? "I've had several fall across the road after I went in. I keep an ax on the back floorboard just in case." He tossed a nod backward over his shoulder, to where the ax lay. Inside, the busy anthill of his brain switched up another point. "Also, don't pick up people or family members."

James blinked, startled at the abrupt turn of conversation. "O-okay?" His eyes scanned up and down the road for said family members.

Marcos went on, not missing a beat. "They don't need to be riding in there unless they work for the postal service. I have seen kids putting mail in the boxes in other areas before, but they are not supposed to be in the vehicle. I can see a kid that is sick missing school, and no one will cover the route, but just for the heck of it, it's not good, plus there isn't much room in here when it's loaded. Also, watch the road good, because a big chunk of a tree can stop your vehicle."

He nearly laughed at James trying to keep up with his mind. *Trees...lumber...random family members, don't pick them up...trees again.* He nodded, very slowly, clearly stumped by the jumble of words Marcos threw at him. "Yeah...sure. Got it."

That's just the way my brain works, kid. Marcos thought. *Probably ought to get used to it, now.*

James slowed a little bit. "I never thought about that happening so much on dirt roads."

"It happens on the paved roads, sometimes." Marcos reached up to grip the handle, resting his arm. "Not as much, though."

The jeep traveled further out of town. Marcos observed James, seeing that he looked noticeably more comfortable. Thirty boxes had turned to 76 in a blink's time. 76 would take a few more blinks, Marcos noted with a quick glance in the back. Attached to a package was the address to box 76, meaning James would have to stop at this one. To make matters even more fun, the dirt road was as narrow as a toothpick, winding back into the forested house. James took his time winding up the road, the comfort easing into discomfort judging by the whites of his knuckles on the steering wheel. The jeep bounced, jostling its occupants like toys on a trampoline as James worked to avoid the dips in the driveway. In the city where houses were a dime a dozen, he was starting to get the hang of it, but out here, where one residency monopolized more acreage than the number of houses there were, he tensed.

Marcos waited until he pulled to a stop in front of the house.

Marcos was tense, but for another reason. He'd traveled this road enough times to know that it was in serious need of maintenance, but there was a reason no one ever went up here. Was James ready for this by his second day? Marcos sent a wary glance to the porch. "No matter what," he said as if James were going in on some sort of life-or-death mission. "Be nice at this house. The man is crazy as a road lizard. He will cuss and yell at you." Not might. Not likely would. *Would* cuss and yell at James. Marcos wondered what purpose he'd find today, other than James being new.

James' face scrunched into an affronted offense. "I won't take that kind of treatment! I don't have to!" Eyes wild with disbelief, he tensed with determination. He reached in the back, ripping the package out from the back. Irritations caused his moves to be jerky. He yanked at the door handle, leaping from the vehicle.

Well. This should be interesting.

Before James could slam the door shut, Gene, the owner of Box 76, waddled out onto the front porch. His body leaned from side to side as he shifted all 300-plus pounds of his weight from foot to foot. His face was already rolled into contempt, as if James was bringing his tombstone rather than whatever he'd ordered from some off-putting Chinese website. Gene's head barely grazed the rafters as his scowl met James.

Marcos sat back. If James was going to blatantly deny what he told him to do and refuse to be nice, let's see how big of a hole he can dig. After all, he doesn't have to take this kind of treatment. He'd said so himself.

Marcos watched warily, wondering if he'd need that ax for more than just chopping timber in the road.

"Good morning!" James called.

Marcos could smell Gene's bad attitude from the car. "What's good about it?" His boisterous voice alerted anyone nearby that if he was miserable, everyone else should be, too. "My back hurts, my hands hurt, its hot, and..." He snatched the package out of James's hands, yanking it out so much that James swayed forward a bit. "You are holding my pillow!"

Marcos' lips pressed together as he tried to dam his laughter behind them. Guess James didn't hurry up fast enough with that package. Did Gene think he intended to keep it?

Gene continued to scowl. "Are you new?"

James's sass and class dissolved into little more than a stutter. " Y-yes."

"It's yes, *sir!*" Gene yelled loud enough to shake the foundations of his house. "If you come flying down that road," he jabbed a finger with the force of a torpedo down the direction where James had crawled down at a snail's pace. "We going to have a *serious* issue! And there is no one around out here."

Was that a threat? Gene continued to blow his stack with the force of Mt. St. Helens. The car angled in such a way that Marcos got a good view of James's face. His snark had dissolved as Gene poured out curses, screams, and other threats. James's eyes rounded, his expression wounded as he stood there like a wet puppy taking Gene's avalanche of verbal abuse.

Marcos decided he'd had enough.

He plucked his car door handle and stepped outside, striding up the pathway. "Hi, Mr. Gene!" He wasn't enabling the man to continue screaming, but he wasn't unkind, either. *Kill 'im with kindness, Marcos. Coals of fire. Coals of fire.*

James turned around to face Marcos, his lip nearly quivering under the weight of his shock. *Thank you,* his eyes flushed with gratitude, and for the first time since they started working together, he appreciated Marcos as his hero.

Gene's lazy gaze drifted over to Marcos. The embers of his rage cooled as he gave a curt nod. "Good to see you."

"How's your wife?" Marcos stopped by James's side, not diverting his gaze to the young man but keeping his eyes on Gene.

"She is doing okay," Gene answered gruffly.

"That's great." Marcos pressed a smile to his lips and eyed his sidekick for the day. "James, we've got to go."

James pivoted and was one step under jogging back to the jeep. He couldn't get away from there fast enough. Marcos glanced back up at Gene and lifted a hand to wave. "I'll see ya."

Gene grunted something, and Marcos deemed it unimportant enough not to request a repeat. He turned to go, when the screeching of a front door turned his attention back around jut as he was about to launch himself into his jeep. Mrs. Lilly, padded her way onto the porch and down toward the jeep.

"What does she want?" James' question sounded less sarcastic and more hesitant, as if he expected another repeat of what Gene had given him.

Before Marcos could reply, Mrs. Lilly's face appeared in James's open window. "Good morning."

"Hi," James mumbled, and Marcos returned the greeting with enough cheer for the both of them.

"Hi, Mrs. Lilly!"

Mrs. Lilly sent a scathing look up to her husband, then back at James. "He don't mean to be like that. He is a good man."

Petrified into both silence and stillness, James said nothing, cemented into the same position like a statue.

"We know, Mrs. Lilly," Marcos assured her.

Mrs. Lilly nodded to James, her eyes filling with worry for him. "Take care, now. I'm going to go start some lunch."

"Sounds good!" Marcos quipped.

Mrs. Lilly began to hobble back up the pathway. James, with shaking hands, burning red face, and lowered eyes, pulled the car into reverse and backed out onto the road. His attitude reeked of being humbled, and Marcos decided that he'd learned a valuable enough lesson and decided to let it be.

James drove to the next box in silence, then the next. Soon, the wordlessness between trainer and trainee became too unbearably heavy, so James broke it. "Why was he so mean?"

Marcos didn't excuse Gene's bad behavior. He didn't know, himself. He answered, trying to keep his voice calm. "That is how he is to everyone except me and two others." The usual cheer was lost to his voice as he respected James's recently inflicted mental wounds. "He has a demon that he just can't shake loose from, I believe."

James snapped around to face him, his eyes burning with the same indignation as Gene's had. "You can't talk religion while working."

"It's not talking religion," Marcos replied in an even tone. "But it is a fact something is wrong with him, and Jesus cast out demons from people that acted just like him."

James gripped the steering wheel, swinging his gaze back onto the road. "I don't want to be preached at," he hissed between tightly closed lips.

Marcos was tempted to become defensive, but that temptation fled when he looked at James, seeing a distorted reflection of himself, years ago. Who knew what this kid had been through? They didn't exactly live in a culture that painted Christianity, and all things pertaining to God, in a positive light. Schools petitioned to take the Ten Commandments off the walls, and campus kids were encouraged to challenge their quietly Christian counterparts. Marcos wasn't surprised that James behaved like many of the youth he'd come across, although perhaps with a little more venom. He didn't condemn him for that, as much as he wondered why. "I used to be just like you," Marcos stated, returning his gaze to the front. He pinched his lips and shook his head. "Didn't want to hear about God. One day, I woke up." He squared James up with a look. "And I pray you do, too."

James snarled, but said nothing.

"You can always come and talk," Marcos lightened his tone a bit. "Gene, he needs prayers. He is one of only a few people that I have ever met like that."

"Whatever," James muttered. He clamped his lips shut, not wanting to continue the conversation. Marcos could practically hear the gears grinding in his head, how to change the subject. After all, they were only to box 80. They still had over four hundred more to go. James waited until he'd shuffled through the mail, stuffed it into the next box, and moved on to Box 80. "So, why is he not that way with you?"

"Well, he used to be." Marcos wasn't going to say he'd never been through what James had been through today. "He would gripe, cuss, and yell every time I pulled up, unless he was gone or his wife was out here. Then, a couple years back, he had fallen through the floor in the house and couldn't get out. I mean he is a big, big man." Marcos demonstrated his circumference with his arms, as if hugging a tree. "I was called out as the fire chief to help. Me and the assistant chief were the only ones that showed up; no one else would. I fully expected to get cussed at and yelled at, but he was, like," Marcos hunted for words appropriate to explain how Gene had behaved. "Docile? Maybe a little scared. I had never seen him like that. As mean as he had always been to me, I helped him get out and made sure he was okay. Ever since that day, he tries being nice, but the look on his face shows how painful it is for him. That is why I say he has a demon."

James' jaw tightened, as did his grip on the steering wheel.

"His wife is the sweetest thing there ever was," Marcos reflected. "She always told me he is a good man, and don't mean to be that way."

"Like she did today," James sounded less hostile the more he spoke.

Marcos nodded. "Maybe that is how she tries to see him."

James clamped his jaw shut until his hesitant voice asked, with more compassion for another human than Marcos had heard from him so far, "Is he that way to her?"

Somber, Marcos nodded. "Yes, he is. He is a mean old cuss."

Silence invited itself into the car, and neither Marcos nor James asked it to leave. In the meantime, Marcos' head spun with their prior conversation, returning back to his inner dialogue with himself about James' hostility toward Christianity. He had to know.

"I am curious."

"Hmm?"

Marcos adjusted to see him better, keeping his posture open, lacking in any sort of condemnation. "You seem to hate the thought of anything out of the Bible."

James didn't deny it.

"Are you an atheist?" Marcos dared to throw the word out there. "I'm just curious, because I have friends that are atheist and some agnostic, but you do seem like them."

James shrugged, his tone clipped. "I just have no interest in church. I grew up seeing people who went to church saying one thing while doing another, and they talked about each other as well. I can't see how it can be real if they act like that."

Marcos had heard the words from the lips of many who had been driven out of the church and away from Christianity because of incidents like that. It saddened his heart – it shouldn't be like that. He didn't blame James for thinking that way. "That's a good point. I have seen that as well."

James side-eyed him. "You have?" Disbelief stained his tone. He pulled up to a mailbox, letting Marcos speak.

"Yes. But I always say a person can warm a pew three times a week and still have residency in Hell."

James paused, setting the mail down on his lap as if the act of putting it in the mailbox required the brainpower he needed to process Marcos' statement. A laugh broke through the surface. "I have never heard that before." He moved, slipping the mail into the mailbox. "Haven't thought about that, either. I bet you don't say that to them." Seeming to find a mutual ground, he gave Marcos the side-eye again, this time with less hostility and more engagement.

"Yes," Marcos grinned and shrugged. "I say that to people."

"Really?" Shock widened James's eyes. "I bet that goes over well."

"Some get rather mad, and that's how you know they know. I don't mince words." He had never been the type. "It's better to show them where they are *not* Christlike than to spend eternity in Hell. A lot of people around here already live in Hell on earth. Many got themselves there, and a lot of kids had no choice in it. A lot of the kids are able to come out of it as good people with a good life. But some won't work hard enough for it, and really can't figure out how, even with help."

James nodded. "I get that. I can see that, too."

Happy to have finally cleared the air on the topic of religion, they continued making their way down the road.

***

James' thoughts were too loud for the radio to drown out on the way home. Happy to be trading Marcos' Gospel music for some of his heavy metal, James tried to headbang along with the beat, but he couldn't quite bring himself to do it. He'd been surprised when Marcos hadn't gotten offended when he brought up the hypocrisy in churches that bothered him. It was a relief not to get hit with the same defenses that he always got when he mentioned hypocrisy. *Don't look at other people, just go for God.* Instead, Marcos had been understanding and didn't deny it. *That's a good point.*

Maybe they butted heads over stuff like this, but at least Marcos had been understanding. James felt like he could plunge into work tomorrow without the dread of being preached at. And if Marcos tried to preach at him, he'd simply remind him of this conversation they'd had.

Chapter 7

Marcos sipped his coffee with one hand, guiding his car toward the post office with the other. He had relived his conversations with James a thousand times since they'd both clocked out the night before. Had he taken any of it to heart? Marcos was grateful he'd opened up a bit and let him in to see what was going on in the kid's mind a bit. He was determined to help him, however that might look.

Aside from that, he'd hyped himself up for work that day. Today was going to be a good day. It was Wednesday. Meaning, they were halfway through the week. Meaning, after today, the weekend would be closer. And it also meant James had two days' worth of training under his belt. Maybe he'd catch on faster today.

One could only hope.

Of course, the pep talk Marcos had given himself earlier that morning lasted all of about five minutes into his commute. Something about the whirring wheels and the workplace drawing closer tended to draw out the negative thoughts and present them in neon colors. James's lack of initiative irked Marcos. He strongly disliked holding someone's hand while teaching them to do their job. At least James had gone through training in Little Rock, but nothing could prepare him for the real-world problems only logic could solve. And a week wasn't enough time to train someone's logic.

Marcos took his time, turning onto the road that ran adjacent to the post office. In the narrow roads of his small downtown town, he spied a semi logger truck, all too big to be poking around down around here, where the streets were barely big enough for one car, let alone two.

"What's that big monster doing down here?" Marcos asked no one in particular, knowing he'd be no closer to getting an answer.

He'd seen the logger truck before. Recognized the logo on the side of the door. He also recognized the method of driving, too. How the logger truck, big enough to take out a house or two in this cramped area of town, paid no heed to that stop sign. Probably thought it was a nice suggestion. Something to consider, so one doesn't cause a collision.

Too much time as a first responder had taught him that it was better to avoid an accident than try to be right. Marcos eased to a stop, knowing it was better than the logger truck would do for him. The logger truck eased toward the stop sign on First Street, closer...closer...

Marcos flinched. The grille of the semi collided with the stop sign, folding it over on itself like a stalk of wheat grass in the wind. Marcos stopped, perhaps a last memorial to the demise of First Street's stop sign.

Metal screamed and groaned as the logger truck continued to drag the stop sign underneath its undercarriage. Ignoring the crunch, the semi made a wide turn, tearing up the grass on the other side of the road, and took a few bites before angling itself correctly onto the road. There, he proceeded to continue driving, as if he hadn't obliterated a safety hazard prevention.

Marcos blinked. All he could do for a few seconds was stare at the poor sign, flattened onto the ground with a jagged tire track slashing through its front. He tsked. Blinked, letting his face twitch off that bewildered expression as he'd watched this unfold before his very eyes. "Well." He settled his coffee cup into the cupholder and shook his head clear of that memory. "Today's going to be a good day."

Wednesday afternoon so far had been wasp-less, Gene-less, and James even seemed to be in a better mood. He'd taken all of Marcos' advice and remembered most, if not all, of it. He remembered to keep the lid on the mailbox at the Robertson's mailbox, checked inside each one for snakes and rocks, and left the AC on full blast when he got to the box where the wasp had made a dramatic entrance into their vehicle. The kid wasn't doing half-bad.

Marcos had held back on the training for each box after the incident with Gene, yesterday. After Gene yelled at James and had a little heart-to-heart about religion, Marcos didn't want to overload James with information. He would rather let the experiences take their toll before piling more on him. His mind was probably too full of the heavy stuff to remember what he'd talked about, anyway. Let him sleep it off.

He picked up where they'd left off yesterday, just after Gene's road, a little further down into the country. The dirt road could hardly be called a "road." More like something carved during the Oregon Trail that hadn't been occupied since.

Of course, it was here, of all places, on a road that looked more like someone's ill-kept driveway, that James popped the question. "Is there a place close that has a restroom?"

What did he think this was, a road trip? Marcos waved his hand, demonstrating out the window. "Look around. This is nature."

James gave Marcos that familiar roll of his eyes, something he dished out at least three times daily.

"But, we can't stop on this road until we get back to the T," Marcos told him, gravely. "Because if you start watching outside, you will see cameras all down here."

He noticed James tense and sent a quick glance out the window, looking for said cameras.

"The people that live here are very paranoid," Marcos said.

"Oh," James mumbled. "Well, that's just great."

"There was a young lady that had your job a while back that I later found out would take a restroom break out here." Marcos exhaled through loosely closed lips. "She sounded so shocked when I said something about the cameras; she had no idea!" He could still see her face. Red-hot embarrassment tinging her cheeks as her eyes looked like she wanted to crawl into a corner and pretend she didn't exist for a while. "The next time I talked to her, she had started watching and noticed several of them. The cameras are on the timberland property, not the property owners that put them up. There are none at the T in the road. It's all timberland property there."

James nodded, eyeing the side of the road for these so-called cameras. "Thanks for telling me. Sure saved me a lot of embarrassment. That poor girl."

"Yeah," Marcos chuckled.

Once they'd finally made it off of the Oregon Trail road and back to the T in the road, James pulled to the side of the road in a turnoff. "I'll be right back," he told Marcos.

Marcos nodded. "Go ahead."

James stepped into the great outdoors, casting wary looks about him before grapevine stepping behind a tree.

An evil idea sprouted in Marcos's mind. Ever the prankster, he never passed up an opportunity to get a good laugh, even if it was just him who was laughing. After giving James a minute or two, Marcos leaned out the window, yelling as loud as he could.

"*Hey! Someone's coming!*"

James grunted in discomfort, hopping out from behind the tree, desperately trying to hold up his pants with one hand. Running lopsided out from behind the tree, he cast fearful looks around him. When he heard Marcos' rolling laughter, he snapped a glare over his shoulder. His irritation became evident in his jerky movements as he realized there was no car.

Marcos kept laughing. James picked a tree and reappeared a few seconds later, striding toward the car. He yanked at the door handle and catapulted himself into the seat.

"No, it was a deer." Marcos grinned.

James did not grin. He rolled his eyes – that's twice today – and put the car in drive.

James was still fuming over the incident at the T by the time they got to box 108. Marcos let him, knowing he'd get over it, eventually. Maybe even learn to laugh about it. When he pulled up to the road, James looked in the back at the oversized package these people expected this skinny guy to deliver. Marcos was sure that two kids of James's size could fit inside. When the vehicle rolled to the stop, four mangy dogs tore off from the front porch, snarling, barking and salivating at the sight of the jeep. James's eyes went wide as he spied them out the door. One dog jumped up onto the door, snarling. He jumped back, despite the fact that the door acted as a barrier between him and the dog. "They're mean!"

Marcos nodded to the blue heelers. "The three blue ones will take a chunk out of you," he said most reassuringly. "But look at the tan dog when it gets close and pet it. It grins. If you love on it, they won't mess with you. They actually get a little jealous."

James' hot glare found its way to Marcos again, stained with a little fear. "I don't like dogs."

"Well," *you will if you want to survive delivering to this house,* Marcos thought. "You'll like this one because it will love you."

With reluctance, James pushed the door open. Amid the snarling of the blue heelers, the tan dog's face appeared in the crack of the door. The head rose up a few inches as the dog crawled up and placed his paws in James' lap. His jowls parted, his eyes lit up, and the dog grinned. It was enough to make anyone uncomfortable, but Marcos had gotten used to it.

"H-h-h-ey, buddy." James stuttered, gently patting the dog on the head. The snarling outside stopped, and the blue heelers appeared out of the windshield, having barked enough to satisfy them, as they walked away.

James quickly got out. The tan dog followed his new friend up the walkway, where James laid the package on the porch. The dog rubbed his legs like a cat, with James stopping to pat its head every so often. The dog kept smiling, and James patted his head once more. His posture was less stiff as he got into the front of the vehicle, closing the door behind him. He grinned, just like the dog. "That is the funniest thing I've seen."

"Isn't it?" Marcos chuckled. "There are two like that on the route."

James stared out the window at the three evil dogs, tamed by him petting a fourth. His head shook in bewilderment. "I can't believe those others walked off and gave up."

"Yeah." Marcos couldn't explain it, either. "They are the only ones on this route that do that."

James eased back onto the road. Wanting to fill the silence, Marcos started up a conversation again. Things that made sense to him might not to James. "If you see money, cigarettes, or anything in the boxes, don't touch them. Sometimes, they make trades."

"No kidding?" James creased an eyebrow, sawing the steering wheel to the right to get the car back onto the road.

"Usually they get it before we come by, but not always."

"What kind of trades?" Naivete tainted James' voice as he glanced at Marcos.

"Well, sometimes pot. Sometimes moonshine. Just don't touch it," Marcos warned, despite the fact that what he was describing was rather illegal. Leaving things in mailboxes, particularly illegal substances, wasn't exactly applauded by the officials. "Also, you will get used to smelling marijuana coming through some places here. There's really not much that can be done about it." Other than wish things were different. Marcos would have loved to have a day when he didn't go down the road, wondering if what he smelled was skunk or some other unpleasant substance.

"Well, the postal inspectors will look into it," James tossed out his comment confidently.

Ah, he was so young.

Postal inspectors? Doing their job? Marcos laughed. "Good luck with that, there. They typically don't want anything unless it is easy, and then have to be bored at least in Arkansas. There is stuff stolen out of the mail system regularly. Mostly packages. They just disappear, and Christmastime is the worst. It is better not to stir the pot. Most people around here are good people, but a lot of them – if you are on their bad side – they will spread the word and make your job harder."

They put a few more mailboxes between them and the road. More confident with every mailbox, James took on a row of countryside houses, each with their mailbox waiting by the road. Waiting patiently beside one of them, a slim woman sent a smile ahead of her.

Cheryl. Marcos eyed the plate in her hands warily, but whatever she was offering in the way of food didn't give him a reason to smile as much as her cheerful disposition did. That same disposition was in her attitude as she called a hello through the open window as James stopped.

"Hello!" Marcos leaned over the console to call to her.

James lost his tongue again, as he wasn't sure what to say. That was fine. Cheryl did a fine job of carrying the conversation with Marcos.

"How is everyone?" She leaned down, peering into the keep.

"Oh, doing just fine. How are you doing?" Marcos threw the question across James' lap. James let them exchange greetings while he did his job.

"Pretty good." Cheryl squinted up at the sky. "I am dreading work today. I know it will be hot inside, unless the air conditioner got fixed."

"Yeah." Marcos didn't envy Cheryl or her work at the small store, selling ice cream in the rear freezers. He enjoyed the ability to get out and about, where each day was different, not stuffed with the same monotony of giving out totals and giving back change in return. The snacks at her store weren't bad, though. "I bought some ice cream there, yesterday, and it was nearly melted by the time I got out."

"Yeah, it's miserable!" Cheryl cried in distress, but quickly recovered as she offered her gift through the window. "Well, here you go. This is better than ice cream, and it won't melt."

Marcos spied a mountain range of cookies he would not be eating under the paper towel. What unnerved him the most was the movement he also observed under that same towel.

"Well, the chips might. Just don't leave 'em in the sun," Cheryl went on to explain. Marcos didn't have the heart to tell her that he would more than leave them in the sun, but leave them to finish baking in the heat on the side of the road as soon as they were far enough away.

James took the plate, obviously forgetting the last time a postal customer had given him a food item. His eyes lit up a little too much, and before Marcos would warn him otherwise, he grabbed one and took a huge crescent-shaped bite out of it. The sewer-fed tomatoes of yesterday forgotten, James smiled in delight. "These are great!"

"They look great." Marcos sincerely hoped James was enjoying them. He really did. Even though the sewer-fed tomatoes would have been far more preferable for reasons James had yet to discover. Marcos was surprised he hadn't discovered them yet.

James eventually passed the plate to him, profusely thanking Cheryl for her cookies.

"You're welcome. Any time. Good to have you with us!" Cheryl sent him a wave. "Goodbye!"

"Thanks! You too!"

As they pulled away, Marcos waited until they were out of earshot before assuring James, "You can have them."

"Thanks." James reached for another one. "You don't like cookies? These even have a crunch." As he took another bite, the crunch filled the car, confirming his statement.

They crunch all right. "I just don't eat hers."

James rolled his eyes. One hand on the steering wheel, the other lifting the cookie to his lips, he kept his eyes on the road. Marcos noticed the corner of his lip turn down as he thought. "I wonder *what* that crunch is."

Marcos sat back, tempted to fold his arms. It was about time he gave a second thought to something he was eating from someone he didn't know.

"I mean," James took his eyes off the road just long enough to examine the cookie. "It looks kinda like..." He thought a moment. "Popcorn kernels."

He wanted to know? "Roaches," Marcos stated as plainly as he could.

James whipped around to face him. At first, horror spread the young skin out on his face, until it dissolved into jest. Probably remembering Marcos's prank from earlier, he spat a laugh, a crumb flying out of his mouth like HAZMAT to land somewhere in the Jeep. "These are great. I don't believe that. Besides," he glanced down at the cookie resting between his fingers atop the steering wheel. "She looked clean."

Just humor me, boy, Marcos thought. With a face as serious as the cemetery they were currently passing, Marcos slowly dipped his head toward the plate on James' lap. More specifically, to the towel wrapping the chocolate crunch cookies. "Open the towel."

"What?"

"Open up the paper towel she had them in."

James sighed. But curiosity got the better of him. Confirming that no one was behind him with a look in the mirror, he slowed the jeep enough to glance down. He folded the paper towel back. Marcos knew the minute he saw it. The disgust returned to his face, along with a shade of green that couldn't possibly be normal for a human being. Something moved within the folds of the towel. Too tiny to be considered adults, Marcos knew that the generous gift Cheryl had given them today was Baby Roach Surprise.

"Uggh!" James exclaimed, tossing the contaminated flour disc outside his window. "*Ug-ugh!*"

"Hey, it's just extra protein!" Marcos dropped the withdrawn facade he'd had while watching James eat the cookies and traded it for a rather ill-timed joke.

One that caused James to heave, apparently.

He jerked the car to the side, giving Marcos a case of side-to-side whiplash. Barely throwing the jeep in park, James swung his door open, raced to the front, and spat out the rest of the chocolate roach cookie.

Then up came the rest. Boy, a sight like that sure gives new meaning to the phrase *toss your cookies.*

Welp, Marcos sat back in the jeep, patiently waiting for Jame to clear his stomach. *Here we go again.*

With no one and nothing but the headstones of the deceased to witness his second loss of dignity, James wiped his mouth and sauntered back into the jeep. He pulled around the mess he'd made, angling the jeep back onto the road. As a finishing touch, he flung the plate of cookies out the window like mini frisbees, littering the side of the road with a minefield of bug biscuits.

"No matter what, you have to be nice to her," Marcos reminded him, not addressing the last five minutes. "She means well, but that was how she was raised and doesn't see anything wrong with it. I have been in her house a few times over the years, you can smell them in there. You wouldn't know by looking at her. She is a very nice lady and would do anything to help someone."

James gagged, his lips and cheeks bulging with a dry heave. It was then that Marcos decided to change the subject, or the entire town of Gillham might smell like regurgitated cookies. "Also, she has never scribbled on a piece of mail that was not hers, nor does she complain about mail that says 'current resident.'"

James side-eyed Marcos, remembering their conversation from his first day, shortly after the first time he'd lost his lunch in the ditch, somewhere. Eyes back on the road. Then back at Marcos. Finally, a laugh bubbled to the surface.

The incident caused James to drive slower, but once they'd reached Box 117, Marcos inserted more commentary to keep James' mind off of the cookies and back onto the job. "I have known this girl all her life," he nodded to the house attached to 117. "I was delivering a package a while back." He began the story in something of a melodramatic tone. "I didn't think anyone was home, which was usually the case. There was no car there. So, I got out and put the box on the grill on the porch. As I was walking away, I heard the door open a little, so I turned around," he demonstrated by turning toward James in the seat. "And it was her kid. She recognized me and said hi."

"Aww," James commented while robotically delivering the mail and pulling away.

"She is real nice, too. I showed her the package and told her to have a great day. Then," he began chuckling before he could even finish the story. "I heard the unmistakable, high-pitched *DING!*"

James's eyes grew wide, and he fought between keeping them on the road and paying attention to Marcos's story.

"I felt a chill go down my spine. Her bat hit the floor."

"A baseball bat?" James cried in disbelief.

"Yep," Marcos' series of chuckles continued. "She was about to get me with a bat until she figured out it was me."

"Oh, wow!" James matched him in laughter. "Just for delivering a package."

"She thought someone was breaking in," Marcos explained. "I was laughing, telling her mom about it later. She said, 'Yeah, she told me about it, and I told her you can't beat the mailman up. I have known him all my life!'"

He and James continued laughing down the road. "It is still rather funny," Marcos commented.

"You gotta laugh at those kinds of situations," James concurred. "After they've happened and everyone's okay."

"Right. After the fact," Marcos agreed.

His story about the baseball bat seemed to restore the lightheartedness to the air for the next seven or so boxes. Box 124, however, brought with it an eerie atmosphere. James didn't seem to feel it, but Marcos had been up this road enough times to double his caution each day he drove it. "Always keep your eyes and ears open out here." He glanced around to confirm his own statement without realizing. "Watch your surroundings; mostly for your safety but also for others."

"Why?" Goosebumps picked their way up and down James' arm. In a hurry now, he pulled up to Box 124 and began shuffling through the mail.

Marcos eyed his surroundings, since James must not have mastered the art of looking at addresses and looking for serial killers lurking in the bushes. "A few years ago in this distribution district, there was a postmaster and a carrier killed by a local person that was drugged up."

James ceased his mail shuffle and darted his gaze up to Marcos. The fear of his life reflected there. "Really?" he quaked.

Marcos nodded. "It was a sad deal. Most people want their mail and get upset about delays, but you never know about someone using drugs, including alcohol." He fell silent, remembering one of the times even his skin prickled and his pulse doubled. "I was right there at that box one day and I thought I heard something. I wasn't sure; I kinda thought it was in my head. So I got still, turned the radio off, and I heard what I thought was '*help*'. As I slowly pulled up, I saw an old man, Johnson, on the ground leaning against his car door."

James paused to listen, his eyes wide, taking Marcos' story to heart.

"I was stunned, because you could tell he had been there a while, and in poor health." Marcos's laughter from earlier faded into a more somber tone. The somberness befit the situation, and he remembered it clear as day as he narrated it aloud to James. "He had slid down getting out, and didn't have the strength to get back up." He'd looked so frail, lying there, baking in the sun. So frightened. Marcos' heart hurt for him, even to this day. "I called 911 and helped him get up. Comforted the best I could before help arrived. He passed on not long after."

James looked down at his lap, quietly, and said nothing.

Marcos let the air sit between them for a heavy moment. He didn't believe in ghosts, but the memories about that day haunted him just the same. "That was probably part of the reason I became a volunteer firefighter and first responder."

"Yeah?" James looked up at Marcos, as if reading his face. James could tap into compassion on occasion. Somewhere hidden beneath the kid trying to learn how to do life was a tender heart.

Marcos nodded. "Doing something nice or saying something nice goes a long way in changing others' attitudes when things are not going good for them."

James's gaze flickered down to his lap again. Likely, he was remembering the incident with Gene yesterday, how Marcos had told him about helping him when he fell through the floor.

Marcos went on, more thinking out loud to himself. These thoughts were his constant companions, so speaking them out loud was like a verbal journal. Therapeutic, in some ways. "We may be the first – maybe the only – people that day whom they can take it out on, or talk about it to. Oh," he added as a bit of an afterthought. "And you are going to hear things you can't unhear. I promise. There will be a lot of untruths, a lot of truths, and a lot of things that are just different."

"I never knew that being a postman could be such an emotionally demanding job." James pressed the gas, having sat too long. He'd probably get a call from the scanner, but neither he nor Marcos seemed to care.

***

James sat in silence for a while, thinking back over Marcos's words. The man was a prankster, no doubt about it. Always looking for a good laugh. After the incident with the outdoor restroom earlier, James honestly thought he was just saying those crunchy – well, he didn't want to think about it – was another silly prank. Too bad it wasn't. But the rest?

James cast him a glance when he wasn't looking, or maybe he did notice, just didn't say anything. Sure, sometimes Marcos rubbed James the wrong way. Religious, sassy, and very no-nonsense about the stuff that rattled James' cage. There was no *sorry, those are roaches.* Just, *roaches.* No, *hey, you might want to think twice about that tomato.* Just *the garden is fed by the sewer.*

But James couldn't help but think about what Marcos was saying about helping Gene, or helping Old Man Johnson. It seemed important to Marcos that the postman was sometimes the only person they got to see every day. Maybe that's why he emphasized twice for all 500 plus boxes, *be nice.*

It made James think. He didn't like the somber feeling that had settled over the air, but it did give him pause to ponder how important it was.

Chapter 8

The mood lightened after lunch. Marcos held his breath until James had crossed over the one-lane wooden bridge, where no one knew who owed the right of way. As they passed over it, he decided to lighten the mood with more commentary. "Sometimes we get advertisements for the full route. Carriers have been caught throwing those bundles in creeks and rivers. Don't do it."

"What?" James laughed, breaking the somber stillness from earlier. "Are you serious?"

"For one, it's not right. People paid us to deliver them. They paid very little, but they paid," Marcos emphasized. "Second, they can figure out which route they came from, and you are the one they are coming for because they know who works what days."

James took that seriously, along with a small dose of shock. "I didn't think about people throwing mail away."

Things out here weren't like the mailroom training in Little Rock. Marcos figured James would learn that sooner rather than later. "Oh, yeah. Just look it up on social media. It's wild. I don't think it's right that these big corporations pay a few cents to mail stuff that people throw away, which makes the postal system less efficient and loses money in the long run. The rest of us pay nearly a dollar for a piece of mail to be sent. It's definitely not a fair deal for the average person."

James nodded. "Right," but his tone suggested that he was far from comprehending some of what Marcos was saying.

"Most of the stuff we get on a daily basis is just junk advertisements," Marcos admitted with a shrug. "Maybe a quarter of the mail is actually bills and correspondence."

"No one wants bills, though," James held up a hand.

Marcos chuckled. "No, I guess not. But don't throw those away, either."

They wound their way through the road, snaking back into the trees. Cicadas screamed their loudest in the overhead canopy, shimmering with golden sunlight and afternoon splendor. They came into a small clearing, with a road that came partially to a T. The wide open field sprouted more headstones of yet another cemetery, signaling their approach.

Marcos pointed them out. "See that cemetery over yonder?"

James perked up over the steering wheel. "Yes. Looks well-maintained." No doubt he was wondering why on earth Marcos was pointing out a cemetery.

"It had a wedding at a grave out there one time, I heard."

James's jaw unhinged a bit. "No way. Really?"

Marcos nodded. "Yep. People are something else."

James awarded the cemetery a look as they passed it. "Who on earth would want to get married in a cemetery? I wonder if it was free." The cemetery disappeared behind a wall of trees, and another mailbox stuck out on the side, disrupting the neat row of pines lining the highway.

Marcos had to laugh at that. "I don't know." He glanced out the window, hearing another chorus of barking, snarling dogs. Mrs. Nikki's box. You could hear your own approach from a mile away.

James slowed the car, eyeing the dogs outside, maybe remembering the grinning dog from earlier. None of these dogs grinned, save to show their teeth. "That's a lot of mutts."

He wasn't kidding. "Usually around twenty of them."

James shook his head, reaching for Mrs. Nikki's mail. "That's too many."

"Occasionally, someone will grease their front end with one."

James cringed, and his face turned that lovely shade of Christmas green again. "That's awful!"

"Well," Marcos shrugged. "That's what happens when people don't take care of their pets." He'd seen one too many dogs who needed a chain, muzzle, and electric fence. They'd charge out of their yards, pouring the coals to it. While James delivered the mail, Marcos squinted ahead. Something snagged his attention, and he had to look twice. In the bright sunlight, it took his eyes a moment to adjust to the pile of rubble. "What in the happy horse manure happened here?"

"What do you mean?" James straightened his back to peer over the steering wheel as he eased the car forward.

Marcos pointed. "Well, there *were* three boxes there on a pedestal, and now there is only one, and it's knee high to a bull frog!"

The closer they got, the closer his observation became evident. Marcos wasn't sure if some 2 am drunk out for a pleasure drive had mowed over three mailboxes last night, but whatever happened only left one mailbox. He had no idea where the other two were. And who thought it would be a good idea to take what was left of the third one and pound it into the ground so that they couldn't even reach it from a Radio Flyer?

James's brakes screeched as he pulled the jeep to a stop. Marcos snatched a paper from the overflowing console, scribbling a little love letter to them.

James eyed him. "What are you doing?"

"I'm writing them a notice that they will receive no mail until it meets postal regulations." He shot a glare up over his writing at the abomination passing off as mailboxes. "They will be calling later, or tomorrow, and it won't be nice. They will be mad about fixing it. I can hear it now." He rolled his eyes. "'We put it back up.'" He imitated a snotty, dry voice. He handed the note to James.

"Are people really that petty?" He unbuckled, opening his car door barely enough to bang against the remainder of the pedestal. He hung out the driver's side, nearly falling a couple of times as he reached down to stuff the note in the mailbox. He slammed the door with satisfaction and swung back in. As he drove off, he closed the jeep door.

"Many people don't take into account that we have to deliver out the right side, and it's very difficult if the box is not at the correct height."

Something sparked in James's eyes as he sent a leer in Marcos' direction. "I thought you said the customer is always right," he teased.

Marcos opened his mouth to protest, trading it for an upturned index finger and a teachable moment. "On nearly everything else, yes. Not this. I'm not getting out of the rig every day to put mail in a box. If I did that for one, then there would be several, and then more. Before long, it would add an extra hour to the day, and we would be late getting back."

James looked down at the mail, taking up space in his lap rather than the three subpar mailboxes. "So, what do we do with the mail for the boxes?"

Let's see how much the kid was paying attention. As a test, Marcos tossed out, "Just throw it out." A grin spread across his face after he said it. He didn't want James to hear it in his voice.

James did a double-take, his eyes round. "Wha..." He stuttered. "What? Why..." His question trailed off as he noticed Marcos' grin. His lips plastered into something of a duck-lip impersonation, and his eyes held that *really?* glare to them. "Very funny."

Well, the kid was listening. Kudos to him. "No, we take it back to the post office and hold it there. Put a rubber band around it."

"Sure." James paused long enough to do as Marcos asked, then continued on with the journey.

James and Marcos drove out of the heavily forested area, breaking into the long stretch of a meadow dotted with trees. Coming up on Box 141, Marcos spied Brother John, a local minister, waiting beside the mailbox and adorned in a suit.

"You're right. You do meet a lot of people while doing the mail route," James agreed before they pulled up to the mail box. The lines around Brother John's face crinkled as he smiled, his blue eyes dancing with life. He leaned down, peering through the open jeep window. "Howdy, y'all."

"Good morning," James greeted him.

"Good morning." Marcos took it a step further. "How's it going?"

"Hmm." Brother John smiled, casting a small glance up at the robin's egg blue sky. "God has made a beautiful morning for us to enjoy!"

Marcos noticed James tense up, but was grateful he said nothing negative in response.

If Brother John noticed James stiffen, he didn't indicate it, but he directed his attention to him, nonetheless. "You must be Marcos' trainee."

"Sure am," James replied, perhaps too cheerfully.

"How are you liking the mail delivery, so far?"

James hesitated. "It's interesting, but I think I can get used to it. There is a lot more to it than I thought there would be."

Marcos hid a smile. *He isn't kidding. Today was evidence of that, alone.*

"Well, son," John pointed across the street. Nestled in some trees at the corner was a church building. "You are welcome to church any time. It's that building right over there. We only go by the Bible. And you can call me anytime," he reached into his pocket, procuring a card seemingly by magic, and handed it to James. "To talk, or if you need something."

"Uh, thanks." James took the card without looking at it. His squared shoulders left no doubt about his discomfort. "Oh, uh, here's your mail." He handed John the clump of envelopes through the window.

"Thank you." John began flipping through the mail, letter by letter, until he came across a brightly colored, glossy advertisement. He took a moment to read it, his face going as white as the envelopes in his hand. He swayed on his feet a bit as if he were about to pass out. "This one is not mine."

James' motions became slow with uncertainty as he reached for the letter.

"I don't look at stuff like that." Brother John's hand trembled as he handed James the pamphlet. As soon as James took it, his pallor almost matched Brother John's, his eyes went wide, and his mouth dropped a bit. Marcos leaned over to glance at what kind of ad could possibly have Brother John look like he'd read a headline about the start of another world war.

A glance at the advertisement said it all. X-rated herbs, eh? "Well," Marcos grinned, humor staining his tone. "It has your name on it."

"Oh, no." Brother John shook his head. And didn't stop shaking it, either. "No, not mine! I don't know how they got my name."

Marcos reached over, plucking the ad from James' pale fingers. He examined it, his voice bouncing off the paper to John's waiting ears. "Yeah, we have some women that received the same the other day, and they were pretty irate. We had a hard time getting them to calm down. One was so loud, I could hear her before I walked in the post office."

Brother John did not laugh. He swallowed. "Please send it back."

Marcos nodded, flipping it into the bin next to the letters they hadn't delivered to the nonexistent boxes. "Will do." He chopped Brother John a wave. "And, hey, you take care."

"You, too." Embarrassed, Brother John backed away from the car, suddenly eager to get away from it. What had begun as a cheerful meet-and-greet by the mailbox had suddenly turned to quite the opposite.

James pulled away, glancing down at the solicitation. "It's not marked to send back."

"I know that." Marcos leaned his arm back on the window. "But we would have been there an hour explaining that, and he would still be upset. We can put it in the recycle. After a few times of him not buying anything, they will probably quit sending them. There is really nothing else we can do."

James nodded, pulling up to another box. "Oh, okay, I get it." He blinked, bewildered, trying not to look at the ad as he reached for the next set of mail. "How do they get that stuff?"

"The best I can tell?" Marcos explained. "Each time people get those solicitations, they are ordering vitamins and herbs online, and whoever they are buying from must sell their addresses."

"Ah." James pulled away from the box and switched on his turn signal. Sarcasm replaced the shock in his tone. "That's nice." He muttered his sarcastic reply as he turned onto Silver Mine Road. Marcos pointed at the first mailbox. "The next two boxes never mix up their mail."

"Great." James braced himself to try and figure out how to stuff a bundle thick enough to be two weeks' mail into a box already bulging.

"The women hate each other to the point they would destroy the other's mail and such," Marcos said by way of explanation.

This piqued James' curiosity as he slowed the jeep. "Why do they hate each other?"

"Well, they used to be best of friends." Tale as old as time, Marcos added silently. "And the husband of the first box got the second one pregnant."

James' eyes grew wider with the information. He worked to stuff the bundle of mail into the overflowing box.

"Both got divorced, and the women stayed maybe for spite. To make matters worse." Marcos untangled the words in his mind, choosing how best to explain the predicament. "The first box is Richardson. The second box is Hendrix. Mrs. Richardson's oldest son and the Hendrixes' middle daughter are married and live three boxes up." He pointed up the road. Three driveways down, the drama continued. "The kids are so nice, but they don't have big family gatherings as you can imagine."

James' laugh sounded like both acknowledgment and humor. "I bet. Although that might be interesting to be at. The family gatherings, I mean."

Marcos echoed his laughter. "Yeah, 'till the hair and claws came out."

"How close are their houses?" James lolled to a stop near another mailbox.

"I don't know, maybe a couple hundred feet," Marcos guessed. "Mrs. Richardson was always real nice 'till she found out about what her husband was doing. Now she don't like men."

"How did he get by with it?" Enjoying the gossip, James delivered the mail and pulled out onto the road, multitasking his questions with driving.

"I was told by her that he would say he was doing something with Mr. Hendrix," Marcos recalled. "But one day, Mr. Hendrix called her because he couldn't reach him to see if he could do something for him.

Needless to say Mrs. Richardson went next door and found them together."

"Ooh." James's lips narrowed into a tiny *o* shape.

"I know. Mrs. Hendrix and Mr. Richardson were wearing sunglasses and long-sleeve shirts the next day." Marcos shook his head. "Never takes sides with anyone out here because they will all be mad at you. To top it off, the kids that are married share a sibling."

James' face scrunched in disgust. "That's crazy, like a wild movie or something."

The plotlines for those movies had to come somewhere, Marcos agreed silently. "Yep. But it's Arkansas."

James turned the car off of Drama Road and onto Red Bluff. Knowing the next stop James had a package for, Marcos kept alert. If James didn't want another repeat of the Gene incident, he'd better listen closely to what Marcos had to say. "Say nothing to that man when you deliver this package."

James pulled into the driveway. "Okay?" No doubt he was thinking, *whatever happened to 'be nice?'*

"You can wave, but don't say anything."

Marcos noticed James didn't get his feathers ruffled or protest like last time. So, he *did* learn his lesson. James put the jeep in park and got out, clutching the package. Marcos monitored the situation. Curtis was similar to Gene, mean for no reason, but sometimes one could get by without a hollered insult.

"Good morning," Marcos heard James say. He wondered if he was ignoring his counsel or just saying it out of reflex. He didn't fault him.

Curtis hogged the space on his porch. His rugged skin, bags under his eyes, and hair sticking up like a cactus indicated that he hadn't slept all night. Or ever seen a brush, as long as he lived. Even better, a step up from his tousled appearance, he wore a T-shirt complete with a diaper underneath. He didn't look anything like the younger version of Curtis Marcos knew, who would go to bars looking for a fight to pick. Somewhere to take out all that pent-up anger. Now, he just saved it all for the mailman.

James handed him the package. "What are you doing still on my porch?" he demanded when James didn't move off his porch in a millisecond.

James' eyes went wide, and he stumbled back. He slipped the package onto the porch and jogged back to the truck. As soon as he slammed the door behind him, hurriedly closing it to avoid another incident with a mean old man, Marcos kept his gaze on Curtis, who'd found his way to his feet. "I told you. He needs lots of prayers."

James ignored the prayers comment, probably used to hearing it by now. He put the jeep in reverse and backed out of the driveway, back onto the road. "Is he *always* that way?"

Marcos gave a single nod to emphasize his point. "Yep. As long as I can remember. I send him a card once in a while, but I'm not sure if he reads it. Usually, he is in the house, and you won't see him. Just be nice; being nice goes a long ways."

James' lips tightened together. *I was being nice,* Marcos could read on his face.

"His brother lives in the very next house," Marcos narrated as James pulled up to the mailbox. "And you would not know they were brothers unless someone told you. His brother is a hard-working man; always willing to help others, and always clean-cut with nice clothes." Through the trees, Marcos noticed a man standing near his mailbox, lifting a hand in greeting. "That is him right there, waving."

James returned his wave. "Well, do they get along?"

"Yes." Marcos was tempted to add *surprisingly* to the end of his statement, but chose not to.

Leaving Curtis and his brother behind, James took Beller Road. Today must've been a day for postal customer meet-and-greet because next to a box five feet from the turnoff, Mrs. Bonny awaited patiently. Marcos recognized her before they pulled up, a well-rounded woman full of smiles who always carried a scent of delicious cooking with her. Just like with the cookies earlier, she held two plates in her hand, but this time, Marcos trusted the food from her kitchen. Her kitchen boasted no cockroaches and food that kept you coming back for more. James pulled up to the mailbox just as she leaned forward. "Good afternoon," she greeted.

James echoed her greeting robotically. "Morning!" Marcos called. Along with the pies, Mrs. Bonny always offered more than a slice of cheerfulness, which in turn brought a ray of sunshine to Marcos' day.

Mrs. Bonny's hands each contained a plate of tempting chocolate pie slices. She leaned down into the open window, her eager face appearing just under the roof of the car. "I just wanted to meet the new fellow."

James glanced up, awkwardly, as if expecting to get bombarded with questions as he normally did. But Mrs. Bonny surprised him.

"Are you liking it so far? It's not too overwhelming, is it?"

"I'll get used to it," James evaded.

"There's a lot in life that takes some getting used to," Mrs. Bonny encouraged him. Kindness seeped into her blue eyes as her voice softened. Marcos sat back, knowing he could safely leave James in conversation with Mrs. Bonny. She wouldn't tear into him like Gene or Curtis would or flirt with him like Mrs. Reynolds. "But the more you push through, the easier it becomes. You've got you a good teacher, there." She nodded inside to Marcos.

"There's a lot to learn." James handed her the mail, then pulled it back, realizing that both her hands were full of the pie slices. "And a lot of things that I wasn't expecting."

"That's just part of the fun," Mrs. Bonny laughed. "Here. This'll help. I made them with you two in mind." She handed the first slice out the window. James passed it to Marcos, then took the second slice. Not as eager to dig into it as he was the tomato or the cookies, he handed Mrs. Bonny her mail in return. "Thank you, ma'am."

"Call me Bonny." Her smile lit up the morning. "And remember, it can only get better from here."

James paused for a few moments. "Thank you. I will."

"Goodbye!"

"And thank you for the pie!" Marcos called out through the window.

"Yes, thank you."

"Oh, you deserve it. You work hard." Mrs. Bonny gave a wave.

They echoed her farewell, then James pulled from the mailbox. Once he was a polite distance away, he handed Marcos the piece of pie. "You can have my piece. I can't trust food out here."

The kid had learned the hard way. Marcos chuckled. "Well, you have to learn the people." But he wasn't complaining. He was more than happy to grab the plastic fork Mrs. Bonny provided and chomp down his piece first, fully intent to devour James' as well.

James side-eyed Marcos once the car had stopped at the next mailbox. "I don't want to know about her kitchen."

Marcos grinned around his mouthful of pie. "Too bad. She makes the best food there is. It always tastes great." And bonus points? No bugs.

James closed the lid of the next mailbox and pulled away. After a contemplative pause, he nodded. "She smelled like food."

"Yep." Marcos shoveled in another forkful of pie. "That is a real woman. She can cook *and* has a clean kitchen."

James eyed the slice of pie, then shook his head. "My stomach is still loopy."

Marcos laughed. "A woman that smells like food and has some weight on her is a great cook. If it's a twig cooking, just leave." He couldn't dismiss the grin from his face, staring at James' unwanted piece of pie. "You will figure out what each person does pretty fast. Nothing is a secret delivering mail; what you haven't seen or heard yet, you will. Every day is a new adventure out here."

"I've noticed." James turned onto Loveless Road. He glanced at the name, his lip curling in disbelief that someone would call out a road name like that. Maybe he was wondering if the road and its residents lived up to that name.

If he did wonder, Marcos wasn't going to deny it. He had stories from this road that caused it to be correctly named. He leaned down to peer out the windshield and pointed upward. "See that house up the hill there?"

"Yes." James followed the direction of Marcos' point.

Marcos sat back "I was right here one morning, and got a call that the man that used to live at that house was unresponsive. So I went on up there, and sure enough, he was there in the yard laid out, not breathing. I checked him out and started CPR. I asked the man's wife, who was there, if she could breathe for him. And – I kid you not – she said, 'Oh no, it might hurt my knees.'"

James choked on air. "*What?*" He threw a momentary stare at Marcos to read whether or not he was joking.

Unfortunately, this time, he wasn't. Marcos nodded his bewilderment, even years later. "She wanted *me* to do CPR on *him*. So, I'm on my knees, thinking while doing chest compressions, *she wants him dead*. I worked on him 'till an ambulance showed up. It was interesting."

"But, did he move?"

Move? A curious word he chose. Marcos might have gone for *live* or *survive,* or even *make it.* But move? He couldn't help himself. "Yep." He pinned James with a stare, ruined by the grin that played about his lips. " To the cemetery."

James rolled his eyes. Wasn't that the third time today? Marcos decided to start keeping a score. James finished up the route on Loveless, then moved on to Blanton Trails. With new roads came new stories, memories firing off like a shooting range. The memory that lurked up Blanton Trails was neither happy nor sad, just different. "This road is a mile in and out, but its narrow and steep. So, be careful. Sometimes you will meet people pulling trailers out of here, and there's no room."

"Got it." James locked his gaze onto the road.

"Also," Marcos nodded as an afterthought. "On the way out, old Three-Legs is going to run out here. He always hits the side of the car while biting the trim on the side."

Marcos could see the wheels turning from the way James frowned, his eyes darting to and fro, as if the answer lay hidden somewhere within the span of the windshield. His lips stalled around the *W* in the word *What,* before he ever voiced the question. "Who is three legs?"

"It's a bulldog," Marcos said bitterly. "And mean as all get out. I call it Three-Legs because it only has three legs left. It done lost one from chasing vehicles."

James laughed, partially in disbelief. "How fast can a three-legged dog run?"

"It's fast," Marcos replied, entertained by the vision of the tripod-dog darting out from his home toward the car, as if he could somehow take it on. "Believe it or not, you will see. Never stop or pull in. It will bite you, and the tires and your car."

"Nice dog," James said with bitterness. "Why don't people keep their dogs up?"

"That's a good question, but folks around here don't."

James remained tense until the end of the road, turning around where Marcos instructed. Just as he put the car back in drive to leave this route behind, James did a double-take at a spot behind the trees.

"There's a glimpse of red there..."

His voice trailed off as the dog burst through the driveway, thus answering his unfinished question. Amid ferocious barks and snarls, the tripod-dog flew toward the jeep. Just as Marcos predicted, he disappeared from view, and a loud *thud* hit the side of the car. James jumped, startled. No matter if it was expected, hearing something hit the side of one's car was always unnerving. "I thought he was coming inside for a minute! Dang, he can run!"

Marcos leaned out the window, seeing the bulldog eating their dust in the rearview mirror, barking his silly head off. "I think it runs faster with three legs than most do with four."

James didn't disagree. "That's crazy!"

Marcos nodded ahead to their next destination. "Last week, its buddy bit the dust on Old Beller road. It wasn't as fast."

Continuously throwing glances in his rearview mirror, James shook his head, bewildered. "Why would they keep a dog like that?"

"Well, they say it don't bite," Marcos replied with enough disbelief to tell James the truth. "But I'm not sure *what* it don't bite."

Turning back onto Old Beller Road, James paused to open the Hinton's box. He stopped abruptly from putting the mail in. Hard to stuff mail in a box so full it would be bulging at the side if this were a cartoon. "What is going on, here?"

"Just wiggle some room, and put it in," Marcos instructed. "I'll send him a message later."

James began to wedge his fingers between the envelopes, finding it difficult to force even his fingertips through. "How often does he check this?" Marcos could almost hear the *once a year?* tacked on to the end of his inquiry.

He laughed. "When I message him, or bag it up and hang it on his door right there." He nodded to the front door.

James frowned, barely making a space between his thumb and forefinger to stuff in more overdue bills. "His box is literally 100 feet from his front door, and he won't check it?"

"Yep." *Welcome to my world, where folks expect you to do all the work.* "And he isn't the only one. It's just the way he is."

James pulled out, stopping just short of a squirrel diving for his life across the road. "Whew," he sighed, shaking his head and easing away from the overfull box more slowly.

"You must watch the critters around here," Marcos indicated the squirrel. "Sometimes they get in the way, especially those two dogs. They bark and chase as long as you are moving, but when the vehicle stops, they stop. Sometimes the critters will get a little mail out to chew on."

James chuckled at that.

"They have checked it more than him," Marcos added, indicating the stuffed full box.

"You can say that again."

James and Marcos made idle conversation once they eased back onto the highway. Marcos could tell James' nervousness pulling over to the shoulder, knowing cars and semis were barreling down at 45 mph behind him. That is, if they obeyed the speed limit through town. Some people felt it was better to maintain a speed of 55 all the way through, regardless of the safety concern it posed. It had unnerved Marcos at first, too, especially being a first responder for so long. He had a laundry list of accidents and several of them on highways just like this. But he'd gotten used to it, and in most places, he was grateful for the wide shoulder.

James breathed a sigh of relief when he pulled off the highway, until he spied the pedestal of 12 boxes in a row.

"Most of the people down there have no idea what their address is," Marcos stated. "The county came in, changed the road name, gave everyone new addresses, and didn't notify us of the changes."

"Well, that's nice," James began with the first box, double-checking the so-called addresses on the envelopes.

"That's what the people here thought. Not even the people who live down this road know. There are a couple of people that just moved there that gave us the new road numbers, but we can't verify anything because the county coordinator isn't coordinated enough to send the list to us."

James breathed a laugh at Marcos's choice of words. Marcos noticed he hadn't even started putting the mail in the boxes, just stared at the addresses, trying to compare them with the mailboxes. It wasn't just him. Even Marcos had to work to decipher the mess of mailboxes in this area.

"It's been at least two years since they changed it. These boxes don't have the right numbers. You just have to get it figured out the best you can for now." Marcos understood the confusion that stumped him even after 16 years of mail delivery. "Under no circumstances ever go down that road. It's terrible! It's not maintained, and the people don't expect us down it."

"Well, that's good, then." James took Marcos' advice and did his best with the mail numbers in the mailboxes.

"Nothing is numbered down there either, according to the people that live at the end." Marcos shook his head.

"I thought everything is supposed to be numbered." James moved on to the third box, easing forward ever so slightly.

One would think, wouldn't they? "Well, if I didn't put the numbers on most of the boxes around here, very few would have numbers on them, and that is how it works most of the time. Besides, why would you put your address in front of your house?" Sarcasm dripped into his tone. "I mean, if you had an emergency, would it not be funnier to watch them go to the wrong places first?"

James had to laugh at that. "Right?" Box 6, and halfway through.

"You have to realize people out here are either laid back and easy going, and not worried about their mail. Or, they are paranoid about it, and the paranoid ones usually get a lot of junk mail. Some people, if they don't get much mail for a few days, they will say something to you, thinking you are hiding it." Marcos laughed at a few memories of being accused of hiding someone's Montgomery Ward magazine. "I'm like, 'yep we keep yours hid in special closet, number two, just to make you suffer!'"

Finishing up with the last box, James laughed and eased away from the mess of numberless boxes.

As with all one-sided conversations, Marcos couldn't think of much else to say. He sat alone with his thoughts for a few boxes. Every mailbox, every house held a memory, and one in particular on Rose Lane sparked one of colder days and frosty mornings. It was hard to imagine the chilly winter when the sun beat down on their car, competing with the AC and winning, but eventually the holiday would come around again. Marcos loved that time of year, when the stars shone more clearly because the cold chased away the haze in the air caused by hot humidity. Ever chipper, he'd greeted the owner of the house with a cheery "Merry Christmas," and received a shoulder colder than the frostbitten air. Might be a good time to point it out to James so he didn't receive the same. The kid would run into enough unkind people, if he stuck around. "Do you celebrate Christmas?"

"Yes." James' face lit up. "I look forward to it."

"Cool," Marcos replied. "There are some people that don't. I have them listed in the list. Its not going to hurt to say 'merry Christmas' to them, but don't push anymore than that because it may not go over well."

James pinched a frown onto his face. "Who doesn't celebrate Christmas?"

"More than you think, I bet." Marcos adjusted his posture, half-turning to fully face James. "Why do you celebrate it if you don't believe in God?"

James paused a moment, his face intense with thought. The only sound was the wheels grinding the dirt beneath his tires. "Well, I always have. It's fun to get things." His answer didn't surprise Marcos. "It's not Jesus' birthday, anyway," James added with a shrug.

Couldn't argue there. "Very true. If it were a real biblical holiday, there wouldn't be nearly as many people celebrating it."

"Lots of people celebrate Easter," James pointed out. Marcos appreciated the lack of hostility in his voice.

He wondered if his argument would bring out that same hostility. "No, they worship the Easter Bunny."

He was right. James rolled his eyes and didn't pursue the conversation. Marcos wondered if he was one of these who only attended church around Christmas or Easter. If he did, he probably wasn't very happy about it, but it sparked a question in Marcos's mind. He used it to fill the redundant pulling over, delivering mail, then driving off again. "Have you ever been to church?"

James nodded. His posture stiffened again, and he didn't meet Marcos' gaze, even as he sorted through mail that was already sorted. "A time or two when I was young. But like I said, people said one thing and do the opposite."

Marcos nodded, moving with the car as James pulled away. "Yeah, I see that a lot. Church is a place for rehabilitating sinners, but many can't let themselves be rehabilitated." Curious as to what the young kid thought about God overall, Marcos decided to toss church aside for a moment and ask a bigger question. "Do you believe there *is* a God?"

"Yeah," James' voice wavered with some hesitation. "I think there is something. But what?" He shook his head. "I couldn't tell you what it is for sure."

"Many people study and point out Bible scriptures to prove their points, but they should be studying the Bible to allow it to show them what they should be doing."

James finally met his gaze for a moment as he eased the car to its next stop. Marcos read curiosity in his gaze. "What do you mean?"

"Well, the Bible gives you a descriptive history, and much of it has been proven by historical sites," Marcos replied. "The Bible gives a good guidance to live by. I have actually heard atheists say the same thing, that it makes for a good society. Like the 10 Commandments."

James continued to listen as he departed from the mailbox, turning on his turn signal to take the car down Blue Cow Road.

Marcos continued, seeing that James had no commentary with which to interrupt. "There are a lot of good people in this world. Some are Christians, some are not. I believe God expects us to be good and helpful to others, no matter what they believe or don't believe. That is how I read the Bible, and I believe the steps laid out in the Bible are for us to go by. It doesn't appear that everyone reads it that way, or believes what they read."

"Agreed." James' tone suggested more bitter agreement than warmth.

"But a person can always change while they are alive." Marcos stared out the windshield. "There is hope."

***

James didn't like to admit it. He would never admit it out loud. But Marcos' words kept echoing in his head, and he couldn't help but give them space. It was hard not to believe there was something bigger out there. But he wasn't sure if he believed in the Bible, or anything. Especially since the people who read it didn't always follow it, as Marcos said.

He robotically stuffed some mail inside a box. His thoughts were so loud that he barely noticed the small car zipping toward him as he started to turn the wheel back onto the road. Thank goodness he did, and was able to slam his brakes before it was too late. The car buzzed by, its little motor protesting at the accelerator pushed to the floor. The car angled itself in front of them. James pulled out behind it, but they didn't have to worry about tailgating the car. Its bumper slowly became smaller and smaller as it zoomed toward the end of the road, where a bunch of rich people's houses were crammed.

"They were in a hurry," James remarked. If he recalled from yesterday, the road was only 4 miles, so wherever they were going couldn't be that far. Did they really need to turn this into a racetrack?

"Yeah, that's all the time with them," Marcos replied.

"So you know these guys?" James secretly hoped Marcos wasn't knocking points off his driving record for pulling out before he saw the car. If he was, it was his own fault. Bringing up God and religion into it all, and causing a distraction. Was this going to be a daily thing with him? James couldn't wait to be alone on this route. That is, if he kept the job up.

"Not personally, but I know *of* them. They drive the same car," Marcos responded.

James found himself bored of the redundancy of going from box to box. For the next two or so miles, it was the same thing: pull over, deliver. Pull over, deliver. Check for cars, which he did twice as much now. As he rounded the curve, James pumped the brakes, going slow enough that the mail and the car's occupants weren't thrown forward by much. The corner straightened out again, but James didn't speed up. The road was littered with debris. Skid marks formed little S-shapes, ending in straight black streaks along the road. Surrounding them, pieces of a car, the same color as the one who'd shot by, along with pine branches and needles, lined the area.

"Oh my." James felt horror sink into his stomach. "Was that the car that passed?"

"Yep," said Marcos, gravely. They passed a fallen tree branch, and James remembered Marcos telling him to look out for fallen timber, like this. Even in fancy neighborhoods like this. "Looks like she barely missed the trees, just took the limbs," Marcos went on. "I bet that car looks different now."

Regardless, there was no car with its nose in the ditch along the way, so she must've gotten back on the road and continued driving. James worked his way around the obstacle course of car parts, a fallen pine tree, and a sign that read *Slow, children at play* hanging from the hands of a plastic toy, shaped like a person.

Joke's on you, I'm already going slow.

Considering the number of people who must live up this neighborhood, and the car that zoomed by, James couldn't help but scoff. "It don't look like they take their own advice."

"Yeah," Marcos agreed. "I've been run into the ditch several times on this road."

James was already started to simmer in his brewing dislike of these people. He paused at the third box, but a flash of silver caught his eye. He stopped, taking a moment to examine the scene more closely. There, just out the window, what was left of that car speeding by sat, propped up onto the curb by one wheel. Steam or smoke rose from the hood, and a middle-aged woman stood beside it. Biting her nails, her eyes were wide, and she glanced around nervously.

Concerned, Marcos rolled down his window. "Are you okay?"

"Yes." Her words came out quickly. "Just...please don't tell my daddy."

James tried not to laugh, because the situation called for it. At least she was okay, but, hey. He didn't have to go knocking on this chick's door because the minute her dad stepped out to check the mail, he was going to notice something was off about the car. Kinda like the fact that it didn't look like a car anymore.

"Okay." Marcos rolled his window back up. James finished up with box three, heading for the next one with caution. Marcos leaned over to

James. "Not sure how he's not going to figure that out since the front clip is all over the road."

He had been thinking the same thing James was. A small laugh burst from James' lips. "She looks old enough to know better."

"Yep," Marcos quipped. "She is my age, and that's not the first time she has done that."

James couldn't help it, but he had to know! "Is she not too old to be afraid of what her dad will say?"

Marcos laughed. And laughed. James couldn't help but join him. "Yeah ... it's a long story."

Everything was in this part of Arkansas, James was coming to find out. What a day, man. What a day. He asked, for perhaps the thousandth time since eight am on Monday morning.

What had he gotten himself into?

Chapter 9

Marcos rejoiced when they reached a little corner store along the way. It wasn't a 5-star hotel with room service, but it meant that for a few minutes, he could get out, stretch his legs, and maybe grab something to quiet the growling of James' stomach. "I'm going to stop at the store in a few minutes if you need a snack or restroom break," he explained to James. "But, keep in mind, everything is way overpriced, and the combined sales tax is the highest in the state."

"This little town?" James arched an eyebrow.

"Exactly. We are number one at something." Marcos grinned as he took a jab at the town. "We have to lock the doors anytime we stop, so nothing is tampered with."

"Got it." James turned off the engine. He got out, stretching his hands behind his head before he considered closing his door. As he closed it, he clicked the key fob until it beeped that the mail was secure.

He fell into line beside Marcos toward the small corner store. "I ran over a dog here, one time I was getting gas," Marcos recollected. "It was a stray, but it must have laid down right in front of my front tire as I left. I felt a little bump, and stopped. I was pretty shocked."

So was James, given the look on his face. "Oh, the poor dog!"

"I know." Marcos shook his head. "It makes me sick to run over God's creatures, but it will happen. Just watch for people and pay attention while driving."

After the incident on Blue Cow Road, he was certain James would take that to heart, at least a little bit.

Marcos noticed a man hovering near the front of the corner store. He couldn't be certain, but the rumpled, dirty clothes the man wore and the shriveled appearance indicated that he might be homeless. Not caring if it made James uncomfortable or not, Marcos paused to talk to him. "Good afternoon."

"Afternoon," a scratchy voice answered.

"You just passing through?" Marcos inquired, stopping to talk to him rather than tossing questions over his shoulder as he walked.

The man nodded. "I've been walking since Foreman."

"Foreman? That's a long way, man."

The other direction of where James was from. His sidekick sidled in beside him, shifting from foot to foot and not contributing to the conversation.

"Tell me about it." A cigarette-stained cough emerged from the man's throat. His worn sole scraped the gravel beneath his feet.

"Well, here." Marcos slipped him some bills, the amount hidden in the coil of his hand. "Tell you what. I own a shop a little down the way." He pointed to a rustic building, hidden in the trees. "I'll give you a few bucks if you pick the trash up out there. I don't have time to do it."

"God bless you, sir!" The grateful traveler cried, examining Marcos' gift as if it were gold.

"You too, man. Take care." Not wanting to sound a trumpet to the issue, Marcos left him with the gift and followed James in the corner store.

James was dancing by now from foot to foot. Looking around, he spied the bathroom. "I'll be right back." He sped off like lightning toward the door.

Marcos grinned, approaching the coffee machine. Out of the corner of his eye, he noticed James enter the bathroom. Before the door had a chance to close again, out came James, his face that lovely shade of pale green that seemed to accompany him everywhere he went. Marcos waited as the coffee he'd chosen dripped into his cup. James scrambled up to him, eyes wide with disgust and urgency. He waited until Marcos had gotten his coffee, paid for it, and was leaving the store in their wake. Before they reached the jeep, James declared his reason for urgency.

"Is there anywhere we can stop? I need to go!"

Didn't he just visit their restroom? "We can go back to the store," he suggested.

"*No!*" The word burst from James' mouth like a torpedo. "That was so nasty!" He gagged a bit. Was this going to be the third time he'd lose his dinner? Poor kid had nothing to lose, now. "Have they ever cleaned it?"

Marcos couldn't help but laugh as he slid into the front seat. "Not sure. I never go there." For reasons.

Disgust lined James's face, and he looked ready to storm the corner store and demand answers.

"Switch. I know a place."

After doing a Chinese fire drill, Marcos casually walked and James danced to the other side of the car, and Marcos drove a few feet before pulling over at an old shop. "There you go."

Pain twisted James's face, but he stopped to ask. "Will we get in trouble?"

Marcos shook his head. "This is mine, this is where I stop."

James spilled out of the car in a tangled mess of arms and legs and ran full-tilt toward the shop.

Safe to say, it was a well-needed break.

Once James returned, he and Marcos took some time organizing the mail for the last half. With a clean bin and refreshed spirits, they pulled back onto the route.

James stopped at the mailboxes along the highway as Marcos placed his elbow in the window crack, looking out. "I drive this area here a lot. I often think about life because it's so beautiful."

"Yeah?" James stole as many glances toward Marcos as he could while still keeping the jeep safely on the road. He turned around where Marcos indicated it was safe to do so and began back the route they came.

"Since I started doing this," Marcos gestured along the road, indicating the mail route, "More people have moved in, many have died, and many have grown up. It seems like only yesterday that I started."

James nodded in agreement. "It is beautiful, with the hills."

Marcos' shop came back into view, a reminder of earlier when it was the only place to provide refuge. As they passed, the homeless man Marcos had helped trudged along the side of the road, headed for the shop. His eyes scanned the ground as he intently looked for something. James did a double-take. "That's the man from the store out there."

"Yes." Marcos thought back on his interaction with the man. "I gave him a few dollars to pick up any trash in front of it."

James blinked. Marcos could see the wheels turning, seeing as how they'd just been there. "There is no trash."

Marcos nodded. "I know." He settled to look ahead, plotting the rest of the mail route in his head, in tandem with thinking over the situation. "God has blessed me richly, and I like to help others. God will bless you greatly the more you bless others, and that don't always mean money."

The talk of God made James' jaw tighten, but his lips closed to any further protests. They'd gotten past the hostility of the conversation at least.

Marcos took that as a chance to go on. "When I was your age, I was invincible." He swiped his hand through the air. "Nothing was going to happen to me. I could do what I want. I didn't want to hear about God. I would always go the way I wanted. And in my mid-20s, I stopped. I looked at my wasted life and began to pay attention to the way God was laying out for me to go, rather than what I had been doing."

James continued listening, popping mail in the mailboxes and leaving them behind for tomorrow's work. He didn't protest.

"I have worked on people I went to school with that had overdosed and heart attacks." A few faces came to Marcos' mind, and he shook his head, wishing he didn't have to. "I hope one of these days, you will do the same. I mean, listen to what God wants you to do."

James didn't reply. Maybe he'd run out of retorts. He turned Marcos' words over and over in his head, at least giving them a second thought rather than just tossing them out. He turned up the road, still having said nothing. Marcos took it as a time to move on. He pulled up to the box and reached around into the back. Hearing a small sigh, Marcos followed his gaze, reading the same address on four or five different boxes. James didn't bother trying to wrestle them into the front seat, so he got out.

"Put them on the table on the porch," Marcos called to him through the open window. He glanced up at the house, chuckling. "He will probably ask you about several packages that are lost in Shreveport at the distribution center. Just tell him it's your first day, and you don't know." First week, first day, who knew the difference?

James nodded. "Got it." Before he could get all the boxes out, Henry stepped out onto the old wood. He hobbled down the porch steps and approached the jeep. The hat with a sagging brim matched his coveralls. The only thing missing was a straw between his teeth, Marcos thought. Other than that, he was a good old country boy who loved shopping online.

"Morning," he called out the window.

"Good morning," Henry greeted James.

James returned his greeting, passing the mail and packages to Henry. Henry read the labels meticulously on each one. "Looks like I'm missing a couple. I'm expecting one from, eh," he rattled off a name Marcos couldn't quite hear.

James handed him the last of his mail. Marcos leaned out the window. "Man, you know they are still in Shreveport. I'm sorry."

"Okay." Henry sounded disappointed. "I wish they would get here soon." He didn't give the ones he did receive a second glance as he looked at James. "So how do you like the job so far?"

"Uh, well. It's interesting," James said with a laugh.

Henry's grin broke out on his face. "Aw, don't worry 'bout us. We typically don't get more than 20 packages a day. That is, if they show up."

Any jab at the Shreveport center he could make. Marcos grinned.

"Now," Henry went on. "If you shoot a deer while you delivering mail, bring it by and I'll help you field dress it, and it'll be here when you get done."

James laughed awkwardly as he slid into the front seat of the car. "Yeah. Um, thanks. That's great to know." He shot Marcos a bewildered look. *I thought he said he wasn't weird!*

Marcos smirked. "We'll see about that when hunting season comes around. Take care, now!"

"Buh-bye!" Henry lifted his hand in a wave. As James pulled away, a toothy grin was plastered on his face as if he didn't want Henry to read his lips. Nothing but a smile. "He was nice...but was he serious?"

City boys. Marcos laughed. "Yes, he is nice and serious. But don't be bringing no gun and hunting."

James nodded in complete agreement. "Oh, I won't. That's illegal, right?"

"Yes," Marcos replied, gravely. "Illegal in several ways. Henry is nice and is easy-going. He don't like going to town."

"I can't say as I blame him." James pulled up to the next house.

And speaking of nice?

Marcos eyed the house, keeping still as he commented. "This next house with a package is so nice it's scary."

James hesitated. "Great. They're either not nice at all, or too nice!"

"Nothing ever dampens their spirit. And you will see them regularly. They have packages every day unless they are lost in Shreveport."

As James parked the car, a man skipped outside, his gait as upbeat as the smile playing across his face. Enthusiasm oozed from him, tangible enough to feel through the windshield. "Good afternoon!" he greeted James as if he were bringing him wonderful news. "I'm Steve. You must be the new guy!"

"I'm James," James attempted to match his enthusiasm and fell short.

Steve's grin never wavered as he eagerly shook James' hand. "It's a wonderful day God has made! We're so glad you've joined us. Hey," he pointed to the house behind him. "You can leave packages by the front door if we are not here."

"Good to know," James handed the package off. "Thanks. Enjoy, man!"

"Wonderful to meet you, James!" Steve cut Marcos a wave. "Marc!"

Marcos karate-chopped him a wave as James crawled back into the seat. He shut the door behind him, pulling back out of the driveway. "He was real nice."

"His wife is the same way," Marcos agreed. "They enjoy life and make the most of it. I know I don't come off as friendly, but I spend every last minute of the day enjoying it. I don't let people get me down because they can be miserable all they want, but I don't have to be like that. That makes each day better."

James tilted his head. "I never thought about it like that."

Chapter 10

Gravel crunched under the tires as James pulled into a familiar-looking drive. Rosco Lane had that sense of home, that familiarity where every tree was memorized and the look of one's own driveway so familiar.

As James pulled the jeep into park, Marcos nodded to the package he'd spied earlier that morning. "Scan my package 'delivered,' and throw it in the back." He nodded to the back seat, eager to take his own package home.

James looked up. "So, that's your house over there?" He nodded to the house.

"Yes." Marcos gestured to it with a nod. "The painted one."

"Huh. I never thought about delivering your own mail before." James reached around into the back, grabbing Marcos' package. He set the scanner to it, doing a double-take as he read it. Marcos watched as he brought the package closer to view it, suddenly bursting out laughing. He laughed so hard, Marcos heard a wheezing grind in his chest. "Hey." He angled the package to face Marcos and pointed. "*Hot Cheeks?*"

Marcos grinned, chuckling, but not as hard as James laughed.

"Why does it have 'Hot Cheeks' on it?"

"I filled in the second line on my order form several years ago with that, and it's still there." Marcos enjoyed the laughs he got out of everyone. "It always catches people's attention. FedEx and UPS drivers love it, too."

James couldn't stop laughing. Marcos shrugged, palms facing upward. "Hey, people notice things like that!"

Tears rolled out of James' eyes from laughing so hard as he tossed the hopefully not fragile box in the back and headed out of Rosco Lane. By the time they'd reached the Bull Smith house, he'd finally gotten control of himself and seemed to enjoy his job more than the meticulous frown he'd squired.

"As we pull up," Marcos sounded like a mischievous boy, spilling a funny secret. "Watch the door on the house."

James did.

"Its decorative glass, but you can see them watching through it."

"I see the outline of someone," James started to point, then realized they were watching him and rubbed his nose instead.

"Every day you will see that," Marcos assured him.

"How do they know we are here?" James eased to a stop.

"There is a monitor behind us that beeps in the house when someone pulls in here." Marcos leaned his head backward. "If they have a package, lay it on the porch. They don't come out 'till we leave."

"Kinda like that guy on Monday," James referred to the man who mirrored their actions entirely, by going back inside the house when Marcos had backed up.

"Yeah, except if the dog is loose, don't get out because it *bites*." Marcos spewed the word *bites* bitterly from his mouth, with almost as much vitriol as James had spewed the roach cookies. "I know!" He rubbed his ankle, trying to ease away the memory... "If the door is open when we pull up, they close it. Some people are different around here. Most of the time you won't talk to many people, but since we are running a little late, people are looking for their mail and are expecting to see the new guy."

"That makes me feel so good about myself," James muttered as he closed the mailbox lid, then drove off.

Another half-mile down Fast Rabbit Road passed in relative silence, save for the crunching of gravel under the tires. James looked like he was easing into the routine of his day, his posture less stiff and his motivation sluggish. The trees on the left side of the road parted, revealing a small white house with a mailbox nearly at the front porch. Marcos never envied the girl, Synthia, who lived there, having to share her driveway with parts of the road. But it made delivering her mail easier.

On a bright sunny day, she sat in a chair outside. Her long blonde hair caught the sunlight in a shimmer, and her gentle face looked up as James eased to a stop beside her mailbox. Cradled in her arms was a baby.

James' posture suddenly no longer slouched. He perked up, as if someone offered him his favorite hobby dangling by a fishing line in front of him. His eyes magnetized to Synthia, and he slowed the car more than he normally did. It took twice as long to ease up to the mailbox, which gave Synthia time to stand. Pinning the baby against her hip with her left arm, she waved with her right. Her eyes danced, sparkled.

And caught James's eyes, as well.

Marcos jumped in before he could hand his phone number out the window along with Synthia's mail. "Good morning!"

James took in a breath to say something, but her laughter cut him off. Her laughter was as gentle as a babbling brook. "It's not morning."

"Well, it seems like it!" Marcos joked. James squirmed. He could've delivered the mail by now, but he was taking his time getting it out of the tote. He opened his mouth again, but Marcos cut him off. "We are running late."

James cleared his throat and raised his chin. "My name is James." His voice came out wobbly.

Synthia directed a polite smile to him, nodding her head like a princess. "I'm Synthia. It's good to meet you."

James squirmed again.

"You're the new relief for Marc?"

"Sure am." James plastered on a flirtatious smile so fake that it made Marcos cringe.

"Well, it's getting to be summer." Synthia began. "And my baby will be outside playing. Just watch out for her."

James blinked, nearly affronted that she didn't return his flirtatious endeavor.

"How old is she, now?" Marcos asked. "A year?"

Synthia shook her head and bounced her baby on her hip. "No, she will be a year and a half in a couple of months."

"Oh wow, she is growing up!" Marcos grinned. "I remember when *you* were little playing."

James shot Marcos a small side-glare, as if Marcos had stolen his conversation from him. Not that he'd had much of a chance of one to begin with. Synthia had completely bypassed his flirtation and shut it down. Good move on her part.

Synthia laughed again. "Yes; you've been the mailman a long time."

Marcos increased the volume of his laughter. "Hey, now, you are making me sound old!"

She ended with a series of giggles. "Well, it's good to see you."

"Take care, now."

"You too," James said awkwardly. "I hope to see you, soon!"

"Nice to meet you, James." Synthia waved, then turned her back to the car. Seeing there was no chance of asking her out on a date, James pulled away. Before they even reached the next mailbox, James blurted out,

"Is she single?"

"She is just as well." Marcos wasn't sure if he wanted to reveal that information to James, but he had to be honest. "The baby's dad is a deadbeat and doesn't help with anything. Like a lot of girls and women, she wants bad boys, and she and the baby pay for the effects of it." He shook his head. Synthia was such a nice person, but she made so many wrong decisions. It wounded him to think of it. "She won't listen to any advice. God loves us, but people forget about Him. That baby is a gift from God and deserves every chance possible."

James had gotten good at steering the conversation as far away from God as he could get. "Is she outside, much?"

Baby's daddy is a deadbeat. She doesn't listen. God loves her, the baby is a gift from Him, and deserves a chance at a better life. James had heard none of that. Not a word. Why ask if he wasn't going to listen to the answer? Marcos rolled his eyes. "No."

"Well, does she get big packages?"

The guy just wouldn't quit, would he? "Sometimes. But that fellow of hers is usually there because he's too lazy to work." He didn't recommend that James flirt with Synthia when he was around, anyway. "I mean, he makes three of you."

James let the comment settle, obviously thinking all his scrawny glory could stand up to some brick building. He thought for a few moments, quietly to himself. "He might leave."

Marcos' throat tightened with unspoken retorts, and he let the conversation die, driving on into silence. He was grateful when they approached the Mitchells' box and could move on from Not-Single Synthia. He scanned the yard, spotting a tiny little ankle-yapper, and pointed him out to James. "That little yapping mutt there is mean. I had it dangling off my leg before when I left that porch."

"Yeah?" Clearly disinterested and still thinking about Synthia, James delivered their mail.

"They were like, 'I've never seen it do that before!' while it was still chewing on me. It's mean!" Marcos had more than his share of the excuses dog owners gave their pets. "Oh, he just does that!" "Oh, I've never seen him do that, before." He shook his head. "Finally, one of them got it off of me. That is one thing that would not bother me, greasing my front end with."

That made James laugh, finally.

"So if it's out of the house, don't get out. If it's in the road, well." Marcos shrugged nonchalantly. "That's your call."

James' eyes widened. "Wow. That's kinda mean."

"It is kinda mean." Marcos let him figure out what direction his comment landed. The dog was mean? Greasing the front end of his jeep was mean? No, what was mean, was keeping a dog that took chunks out of delivery and mailmen and thinking nothing of it. "Dogs like that are as useless as a two-headed toad. Most of the time, people will say, 'Oh it don't bite, it's just misunderstood,' or something like that." Even repeating the comments made his fist tighten in anger. "You will typically find that the dogs reflect their owner's attitude. Not always, but most of the time."

James tilted his head, silently chewing on Marcos' words. "That's an interesting theory."

"Did you see that bulldog laying in that chair the last house we stopped at?" Probably not. His thoughts were occupied elsewhere.

James didn't have to say it, but he did. "No."

"Exactly. It raised its head like we disturbed it and laid back down. Its owners are real nice." He couldn't say as much for most of the dog owners he encountered.

Speaking of dogs, as James turned onto Redneck Road, Marcos inwardly grinned. If James hadn't had enough of dogs as it were, he'd get his fill, here. "This road is just over a mile long, and has around thirty dogs that chase and bite. Keep your arms in and windows up till you stop or you will have dog droppings on you."

James nodded and rolled up his window, no doubt grateful to have a few moments of solitude with the AC.

"Do not get out of this vehicle except at the last house," Marcos went on. "There is no problem with dogs there. The dogs get shot at for killing chickens and other animals."

As if his statement needed evidence to support it, a host of yapping and barking filled the air. Marcos threw a look in the mirror as more dogs than a pound could hold poured out onto the road like ants avenging their home.

James cringed. "That's awful." He, too, awarded a look in the mirror at the mangy mutts chasing them down. "Why do they just let them run everywhere?" he demanded.

"I have no idea," Marcos said. "They don't take care of them, which causes problems for their neighbors. They continue to have puppies, and that replenishes the ones that get run over and shot."

Dogs and more dogs, oh, my. As they finally left Redneck Road after more than a mile of tense hope that they wouldn't encounter a canine and his teeth, Marcos pointed out a new issue with animals, larger than the wolfish beasts. He pointed to the sign reading *Green Acres Road,* narrating as James turned onto it. "You have to watch those horses around here, especially on this road. They are usually in the road or close to it. The owners just let them run loose, and it's nothing to see them a mile from here. If you are not paying close attention you will have one as a hood ornament."

James's silence surprised him. He didn't like comments about greasing the front end of the jeep, so the fact that the hood ornament one receiving no comment surprised Marcos. He glanced over, annoyance resurfacing. He'd thought they were past this. James wasn't even watching the road. Why? He was too busy watching a girl walking down the road to share some of his attention with traffic laws.

"Did you hear me?"

"You reckon she needs some help?" James nodded to the girl walking.

As if he hadn't just said not to pick anyone up who wasn't working? Where was James's mind today? Marcos gave him a hard stare, letting his silence startle James enough to whip around to see him. Only when they'd made eye contact did Marcos emphatically state, "*No*. She don't!"

James tried to look at the girl as they passed.

"You can talk to girls on your own time when you are not working."

James shrugged off the rebuke. "Are they always out?"

"You can talk to girls on your own time, when you are not working," Marcos repeated.

It generated his fifth eye roll for the day.

He passed the girl on foot and the horses that he was bound to hit because he was too busy watching for girls than horses. Another house came into voice and Marcos made a point of gesturing toward it. "That girl who lives there?"

James perked up, hoping that Marcos would say she was single.

He did not. "She is crazy with a capitol *C*. Maybe bipolar, I'm not sure the difference. It's never a good day if you put something in that box other than her name unless she says to, and then she may change her mind any second."

"Oh, great." James read over the mail addressed to her twice.

"You can be talking to her, and she will be just friendly and nice, then all at once, she will start yelling and cussing then go back to normal like nothing happened. So, don't mess her mail up."

"Well, it sounds like she fits in around here," James bit out. Marcos wasn't sure if he was bitter because he couldn't look at girls while he worked, or because he'd encountered so many unpleasant people already. And it wasn't even Friday. "I mean, maybe she and Gene should move close together."

Marcos burst out laughing. "You know, I have thought about that before. Her name is Darla, and she is built like a linebacker. She is tough. She's a good six feet tall and muscled up. She does manual labor, so be extra nice if you have something for her." Images filled his head of Darla tossing James' scrawny form around, like a WWE wrestler. "I have seen her be so sweet, but I'm leery of her; she scares most people and for good reason."

"So," James quaked. "Will I recognize her when I see her?"

"You will." Marcos returned his attention to the window as soon as James left the house behind. "If she is mad for sure."

James pulled up to the next house and checked the manifest. "We've got a huge package for this one," he said.

"Requires a signature, too." Marcos looked over. He glanced in the back at the package half James' size. Then, back at the house. "Have fun. They *may* be here." No sense in hoping for the impossible, though. "I hate getting signatures and postage due. Most of the time, people are not home. If they are home, some don't understand why the package requires a signature, or why money is due, and we don't have the real answers." He glanced back at the house, then did a double-take. He couldn't help himself. He hasn't pulled a trick on James in a minute. "What the heck?! Do you see that?"

His exclamation startled James to look ahead. "What? See what?"

Marcos didn't point. "Right in front of us, between the two trucks."

James looked...and looked. Finally, he zeroed in on what Marcos was pointing at. "...A broom?"

"Yes." Marcos nodded with all the seriousness of a heart attack. "Looks like someone got a new ride."

James blinked, processing the joke before bursting out laughing. Marcos knew he'd agree, with all the people he'd encountered out here. "It don't look like it's been used much. Low mileage, probably."

Marcos laughed. Hoping to have lightened his day a little bit, he watched as James exited the vehicle, lobbing the huge package over his shoulder. He stumbled toward the door, more package than man. He paused to look at the broom again. Marcos watched him. *It wasn't that funny...* that is, until he noticed what James was looking at. The bristles of the broom emitted a grey smoke, smoldering from some kind of fire. Marcos snickered, and from the look on James's shaking shoulders, he was, too.

A middle-aged woman appeared at the door, not caring to have changed out of her nightgown. She peeked through the door. "Hi, I'm not decent!"

Marcos held in his laughter. *I warned him.*

James awkwardly set the package down. "Hi, um. This package requires a signature."

"It does?" The woman frowned. "Why?"

Marcos laughed, hoping his laughter couldn't be heard from outside the vehicle. He could hear the conversation just fine.

"I don't know." James mumbled.

"Huh." The woman stuck her hand out the door. James held the scanner out to her as her shaky hand signed the package. Then, she snatched the package and ran inside, slamming the door shut with a resounding bang.

James blinked, then started trudging back to the jeep. Recalling the nightmare this day had been with James' wandering eye, Marcos decided to test those testy waters. As soon as James had closed his door and put the jeep in reverse, Marcos grinned. "So, how did your flirting go, there?"

James glared at him. "No."

"No?"

"She is old enough to be my grandma."

Marcos chuckled. James glanced back at the smoldering broom. A smile ticked the corner of his lip. "That broom was still smoldering. She must have just pulled in before we got here."

Marcos couldn't contain it anymore. He busted out laughing. "She is a good woman, and real nice. She could be wearing a coat that drags the ground and covers everything but her eyes, and she won't think she is decent, unless she is wearing clothes."

James chuckled a bit.

"Personally," Marcos shrugged. "I don't care what anyone wears or don't wear, I just want to be rid of the package or mail so I can finish."

The route was brought to another delayed halt when James turned up a road. The other half of the road was obscured from view by a train sitting on the tracks. What made it even less desirable was that the train wasn't moving. Just sitting there as if someone had invited it to lunch.

"This might take a bit," Marcos explained, hiding his usual frustration at the train behind a casual tone. "Sometimes we end up going around. I usually give it five minutes. We have to cross railroad tracks seven times each day, and I have a list of where to by pass them if needed."

James glared at the train as the engine idled. "How often do you have to by pass them?"

"At least twice a week at one point or another," Marcos replied, with a hint of bitterness. "And its worse in the winter. I have seen them sit on this section all weekend many times, and it literally cuts the town in half, forcing the elderly and those who walk to go around to the main highway."

"Well, we're already running behind." James muttered, glancing at the clock. "Can you show me how to go around?"

"With pleasure." Marcos checked behind them for traffic.

Chapter 11

Dogs, horses, and hitchhikers, oh, my.

Welcome to the wooded area, where animals roamed free and thought the road was just for them. Feeling like a broken record, telling James to watch out for animals, Marcos nodded to the road next on the route. "Go slow on this road, here. There are very few boxes, but lots of deer. If you're not paying attention, you will have one as a hood ornament."

James nodded, stiffly. "Got it."

Marcos scanned the area, spotting a group of creatures to give evidence to his statement. Well, a group was one thing. This was an entire herd! "Look in the field, up here."

James followed the direction of his point. "Wow!"

He had to pull over, equally as curious as Marcos, why an entire herd of deer could appear like this at any time of the year, except hunting season. "Are those turkeys?" James squinted at the smaller bodies mingling with the ruminants in the field.

"Yep." Marcos wagged his finger at each deer he counted, nearly losing count around thirty. James did the same, but with the turkeys. "I counted twelve turkeys. You?"

"Same. And fifty-three deer." Marcos grinned, sitting back.

"That's a lot of deer!" James exclaimed in wonder, shaking his head. "I thought deer and turkeys didn't stay close together."

"I've heard that," said Marcos. "But sometimes, you will see cows, goats, deer, and turkeys all in that field. These people out here feed the deer, and I mean *feed* them! The deer will follow them around on their side by sides while they fill the feeders up."

"Wow." James carefully eased onto the road again. "That's pretty impressive."

"Another thing." Might want to point this out before James came running back to the post office, claiming he was in a shootout Marcos didn't tell him about. "You have to watch for people driving these roads and shooting at them."

James did a double-take. "What?"

"Yes. And you *will* see them do it."

"Not like that's illegal or anything." James huffed a breath through his lips and took the route slowly.

Feeling the conversation flowing nice and easy between them, Marcos continued. "I found a wallet one time right in here. It was full of $100 bills; over $1000, actually."

"Whoa, really?" James looked all too happy with the thought. If that's what it took to get him to keep his eyes on the road, Marcos wasn't complaining. Maybe he'd drop a wallet out here sometime as a decoy. Empty of course. Maybe with a note inside that said something about *ha, ha, fooled you!*

"Yep. I didn't recognize the name, but I saw the certificates in it, so I knew he worked."

"A little detective work, there," James commented.

"Sometimes you gotta do that," Marcos quipped. "I stopped and asked the fellow at that house there," he nodded to the building in question as he passed. "If he knew the fellow. He said no, but that he was probably up to no good. It did appear the fellow was drunk or something. You could tell he was trying to relieve himself in the middle of the road."

James snorted a small laugh, pulling up to the house's mailbox.

"The wallet was right there." Marcos leaned forward toward the dashboard and pointed on the road. "The fellow that lives there said, 'You can take it to the sheriff's office, they can find him.' I knew that if I did, he would probably not see some or all of that money, and they might not find him. I called my wife and sent her pictures of his IDs.

She searched the internet, social media, and such, and found him that way."

"See? A detective!" James called out cheerily as he left the house behind.

"She sent him my number with, 'if you are missing something, call', with the number. It wasn't long before I got a call. He was hungover, barely functioning, and scared because he needed those certification cards to go back to work that day. The fellow lived over in Oklahoma. His brother brought him over that afternoon. I had a good talk with him about life and choices."

James' laugh indicated he had no trouble believing that.

"He was surprised that the money was there," Marcos remembered. "His brother told him to give me some money for getting it back to him intact, because most people wouldn't have. I didn't take anything for finding it and returning it the way I found it. Taking anything wouldn't be right; giving it back was the right thing to do. I let him know he could reach out to me if he ever had any questions about life."

Marcos let himself drift backward into memory lane a bit, regressing from the current life lesson to the day that he'd gotten that text message later that week. "A few days later, his mother messaged me." He chuckled a bit. "I started cringing, because typically that's not good."

James shared his laughter.

"But she thanked me for finding it and returning it to him. I was expecting to get an earful for talking to him about life, because that is what parents usually do to someone trying to help their kid. But she didn't. She actually thanked me for that, too."

James let the wheels turn, churning into the silence as he moved from one road to the next. "You didn't take any of the money," he said more as an observation than a question. "That would have been tempting."

Marcos shook his head. He may be a prankster, but he wasn't a kleptomaniac. "No. It wasn't tempting, because it wasn't mine and that was the right thing to do." He shifted back into the present, eyeing James out of the corner of his eye. "Always keep a clear mind and a clear conscience."

James had no comment for that.

A few boxes later, the road curved into an unknown path. Marcos pointed again. "There is a brown box up here around this curve."

"Yeah?"

"It has a bird's nest in it with a bird in it," Marcos explained, casually. "Let the bird fly out before you put the mail in or it will be in the truck."

James blinked, as if trying to process how normal it was for birds to make their homes in boxes down here.

"It is a pain in the rump roast to get out." Marcos knew from experience a time or two. It wasn't like cranking up the AC would do the trick as it did for wasps.

James idled up to the box in question. "Wha—. It don't have a lid! No wonder it has a bird."

"That's how they want it." Marcos shrugged.

James patiently waited, rolling up his window for the terrified bird to make its grand, feather-shedding escape. Chirping in horror, it disappeared over the roof of the jeep briefly, before it sailed along the ground in the field across the street.

"So we just...put the mail next to the bird's nest?"

"Yep," Marcos answered. "Pretty much."

James used the bird nest as somewhat of a bookend, squishing the envelopes between the thatch of twigs and lint. Checking one more time for the bird, he made his way further down the road. Just a house or two ahead, the trees spaced themselves out, making room for the house to be seen, tucked back in the clearing.

"A year or so ago," Marcos nodded to the clearing. "Right up there where the clear cut starts, there was a chick who had driven her husband's new truck part of the way in that clear cut, chasing a rattle snake."

James laughed. "A rattlesnake? Oh, this can't end well."

"I stopped and got out to see if she was okay." Marcos could still see the truck angled into the grassy spread. "She was looking around and in front of the truck and said, 'There was a big rattlesnake crossing the road I was trying to kill.' I stared at her for a moment, letting that settle in my mind, and finally said, 'Well, did you get it?" She said, "No, I don't think so." Marcos chuckled. "I really wanted to tease her about it being in the truck, but it was bad. I could not see her husband being thrilled about his new truck with the new design in the front."

James laughed. "I bet!"

"I asked if she needed help getting out. She said, 'No, it's Four Wheel Drive.' So I left before her husband came by."

"I would have, too!" James chuckled.

"They were not married much longer."

James's laughter increased as he shook his head. "I wonder why."

The road turned into the next one for the route, and the usual, yet annoying sound of yapping dogs filled the air. James slowed, sighing as a pack of domesticated dogs surrounded the jeep. "What is it with people and these.."

Buh-bump!

Marcos tensed, letting the noise settle a moment. *Oh, lovely.* James froze, his eyes wide. Horror stretched his face thin. He composed himself long enough to ask as calmly as could be, bracing himself for the answer, "Was that a dog?"

Marcos strained against his seatbelt, looking through the seats through the back windshield. His eyes instantly magnetized to the bump in the road. Oh, boy. *This'll be fun.* "Yep."

"Oh." James cringed. Marcos wondered if he was praying for the first time ever, even if it was for forgiveness.

Marcos couldn't even remember the first time he'd hit a canine or some other animal. It was normal to him. Calm as ever, he turned back around to face the front. A low, staccato tone merged from his lips, quiet at first, but gradually increasing in volume. "'Another one down, and another one down - another one bites the dust.'"

James wrinkled his nose, looking like he was about to throw up for the third time since Marcos met him. "That's awful!"

Well, time to tell him the truth. Marcos burst out laughing. "No, it was a rock."

"Wha..." Anger brewed on James's face as his lips twitched, pushing together against some retort that probably would have soured the mood.

"What?" Marcos's shoulders plopped. "Well, I can't help it!" He could help his impish grin, either. "Neither can anyone else. You can't have that many animals and have them not get out on the road. If it is one or two dogs chasing a car, they typically stay out of the way and will get used to our driving. When there is a pack of dogs, they push one another until one gets under the tires." He added as an afterthought, "You will find that dogs typically act like their owners." James probably hadn't heard him say that earlier. He wasn't focused on anything Marcos was saying at the time.

James still wasn't amused. He simmered in his disgust over Marcos' ill-timed joke for a few moments longer. Marcos didn't care. He continued talking, as if nothing had soured James' mood. "The chick at that second box hates me for some reason."

James' lip ticked upward with a diminutive grin.

Marcos didn't react. "Not sure why. I don't know her, and wouldn't recognize her if I saw her, but she makes sure to call the post office and complain about how bad I do even when I'm not working."

"Well, that's nice," James mumbled, probably thinking that any complaint about Marcos on his days off would reflect on him.

"I think it may be a case of mistaken identity," Marcos tossed out. "She isn't from here."

James finally spoke up about his true thoughts. Marcos heard it in his tone before he said it. "Are you sure she just didn't find one of your jokes *not* funny?"

Yeah, he should've seen that one coming, after telling James he'd just run over a dog, when it was a rock. And after the incident with the outdoor restroom and...well. He'd just stop there for now. He let it land before chuckling a bit. "Well, I don't remember joking with her, but I guess it could be possible."

James moved on to the next box, still proud of himself at his own insult against Marcos. As he opened the box lid, Marcos instructed, "This next box, get it closed, no matter what, because she will be calling

126

either this evening or next morning, mad to the point the post master comes up and closes it himself."

"That's petty at its best!" James said as he made sure to slam the lid shut, then checked it.

"Also, she will know I didn't do it." Marcos nodded, slowly to bring his point home. "You can ask Lizzy about that. She worries about that box, but not when I'm working."

James pulled away from the box. "How does she know it's not you?"

"Because she knows I always get it to shut," Marcos answered. "It's a touchy box when the sun is out and hot. I don't know if there is any other reason she knows I get it shut or not, but I don't ask questions."

James shook his head, moving on to the next box. "That is strange."

As they neared the end of the road, Marcos nodded to a pullover spot. "If you want to pull over here, we'll switch and I'll drive the rest of the route."

James paused, with the tension of a jack-in-the-box. "You sure?"

"Yep," Marcos nodded. "Don't want to wear you out too much the first couple of days."

James hesitated once more before he pulled over to the side of the road. "Thank you." The relief in his voice was palpable.

Heat flooded the car on Marcos' side as he swung the door open. A blast of hot air from the car's grille met him as he crossed paths with James at the nose of the jeep. Once he'd swung himself back inside and slammed the door, he took over the mail route, hoping he could make up some of the time they'd lost.

Marcos did, indeed, make up five minutes here, five minutes there. As he pulled up to a familiar mailbox – not that they weren't all familiar – he nodded out James' side at the window. "Years ago, there was a man that lived in what was a house on your side, where the steps are."

James followed where Marcos was pointing. He focused on the steps leading up to nothing on the side of the road, as if he hadn't noticed them until Marcos pointed them out. Then, he took his time realizing how strange it was that there were stairs, but no house.

"He had moved here from California, and he was a little touched, if you know what I mean." Marcos closed the mailbox with a flourish and left it behind.

James paused for a moment before recognition snapped in his eyes. "Crazy!"

Marcos grinned. "You hit the nail on the head. You would see him at the store in town sometimes, but he seriously kept to himself and didn't seem to be bad." Seems to be. Usually, the words indicated a shift in people's thinking, and certainly, this time they did. "One day, the county workers parked their trucks on the side of the road where we just drove."

"Mh-hm?" James confirmed he was listening.

"They were taking a break or something. If I recall, there were only one or two workers who stayed with the trucks; the others may have been at the store. It was seriously grown up out there, weeds and all, and that guy came out of the brush with an ax and started chopping on the vehicle with the ax."

James' eyes bulged.

"The county workers spooked him, and he hid in the brush, which turned out to be a marijuana crop as well."

"This just keeps getting better!" James exclaimed, propping his head up on his hand.

"The deputies surrounded it, and the county workers brush-hogged it down and arrested him."

"That's crazy." James shook his head in wonder. "What happened to him?"

Marcos returned both hands to the steering wheel as he drove the next stretch between streets. "Don't remember. But I would bet he was sent upriver without a paddle."

He turned onto the next street as James huffed a laugh, then returned his gaze out the windshield. "Still. That's crazy. I don't know what I'd do if someone came at me with an ax."

Marcos drove the quarter mile up the next road, easing to a stop in front of a farmhouse. Caged behind a fence not even strong enough to keep out an intrusive thought, some goats happily munched on the grazing materials nearby. "You must put the mail in the very back of this box," Marcos said, following his own instructions. "Or the goats will eat it."

James leaned around Marcos, spotting the goats dotting the lawn. "Why are they not in a fence?"

That was a very good question. "Well, I can't tell you that. But they seldom get run over. If you have to get out, watch that billy over there." He nodded his head to the devil in question, two large horns protruding upward from his head. "It will ram you. You might call it a guard goat."

Well, *he'd* thought it was funny. James, however, plastered his lips into that thin line across his face and squinted at Marcos through narrowed eyes. "Where do you put the packages?"

Well, he tried. "Leave a notice if no one comes out." Laughing at his own joke since no one else was, Marcos pulled away.

Chapter 12

Marcos knocked out as many boxes as fast as he could, making sure to stop no longer than necessary at each one. He turned up one lane, which always boded ill, and nodded out the window. "This is Badboy Lane," he said. "Do you see what I see?"

James had been quite occupied by his phone, but his gaze flickered out the windshield. It took a few moments for him to spot what Marcos was talking about, as he scanned the area in front of them. "A 'slow, kids at play' sign," he narrated hesitantly, as if he wasn't sure it was the right answer.

"Yep." Marcos found himself pleased with James's observant skills, even if it was something simple such as this. "And some do drive like a fire is under them through here, but if that old man catches you, he will try to whoop you." He nodded to the house as he pulled up. The old man in question glowered from his porch. "He gets mad at fifteen miles an hour, tops. He is serious, even if it's his grandkids who are speeding. Most of the people down here are good, but it's the kids that will run you off the road."

James fell silent. Marcos wondered if he was one of the kids he was referring to. He wouldn't doubt it.

"There are no young kids down here," Marcos added as an ironic afterthought. A sign that announced that kids were around should mean that there were a few munchkins in the area, right? "He is friendly and nice, unless you are driving faster than you should."

"Fifteen miles an hour." James groaned. "Who drives that slow?"

Marcos waved out the window at the old man, who nodded his approval at the speed he chose. Marcos pulled back onto the road and moved on to the next house. As he grabbed for the mail, he sent a nod in the house's direction. "That house up there?"

James' gaze drifted up the walkway to the house Marcos pointed out. "Mh-hm?"

"I was right here close when I got a call that the dad had fallen over and was unresponsive. So I went on up the hill since they had mail," Marcos pointed that out, too. "And he was at the table, slumped over and not breathing. So, after asking if he had a DNR, I started CPR." It was amazing the double tasks the post office would throw at you once in a while. "The ambulance finally showed up and did CPR, but as they pulled away, the paramedic never did another compression."

James stared. "So they only did chest compressions when other people were around, but not in the ambulance?"

"Yep," Marcos proclaimed, his tone clipped but this time with sadness. "I realized each time after that they did not continue CPR, thus allowing the people to die. It was very disheartening and wrong." Marcos had the ability to make a joke about nearly everything, except this. There was no silver lining, no joke about the incompetence of people who were supposed to save other people's lives. "They were just there getting a paycheck. So don't get hurt. If you do, don't call for an ambulance. If they don't kill you, the hospital will."

James sat there, stunned. Marcos could see it on his face. Weren't the ambulances and hospitals there to help? One might think. In a perfect world, maybe. In a world where six-figure sums in your bank account every week were dangling in front of one's nose, it's not likely. While James remained shocked, Marcos shook his head, clearing his mind of the memories, and drove on. He needed a distraction, trying not to think about the old man he'd tried to save, who'd been treated as a number by the following paramedics. A distraction. Something, anything. So he chose to educate James on some more navigation. "Okay. Right up here, the road tees, so we turn around."

James nodded, still quiet. Was he wanting to take a nap, or still thinking about Marcos' story about the ambulance? Marcos went on, regardless. This was important.

"Do not ever, ever, *ever* turn around in that driveway, or you will hear about the sky falling," Marcos emphasized each *ever* in an attempt to convey the seriousness.

"Why?" Ahh, so James was listening. Good.

"Those people don't want anyone turning around there in their driveway," Marcos explained. "They say it destroys the driveway and makes it wash out."

James blinked, eyeing the driveways as they passed. "It looks level to me."

"Yep." He wasn't wrong. "But they will call and complain, and the postmaster and others don't want to hear it from them. We can easily turn around out here, but be careful that no one is coming down the road. The couple is really nice, other than the turning around part." It was amazing the triggers these people had.

As he had instructed, Marcos used the *t* in the road to turn around, and begin back on the route.

James hardly said another word as they rounded the corner to the street equaling the one they'd come from. Marcos pulled into the driveway of another house. "Okay. We have a big box for this next house." He remembered from the notes earlier today. "It has a special note to deliver to the side door. Do not go over there."

James wrinkled his nose in confusion, no doubt wondering why he'd disregard a special instruction. He'd find out soon enough. "As far as you can go is the front door. Do that. They won't come out."

James finally voiced his obvious question out loud. "I thought we were supposed to do what the special instructions say."

Marcos shook his head. "Not if it's hazardous." He pulled in the rest of the way and threw the car into park. James wanted an explanation. Marcos figured he owed him one for telling him to disregard the special instructions. "Look at the yard and the side."

James leaned out the window, scanning the ground. Not that he could see the ground. There had to be grass under there somewhere, but it was hard to see, as the entire yard was clogged and littered with trash bags, bulging to twice their size in the heat. And that was the trash that was lucky enough to make it into a trash bag. Some just lay, scattered, causing the yard to look more like a junkyard than someone's humble abode. Metal and car parts jutted up from the pile, piles of wood scattered on top of other unidentifiable substances. The trash piled up against the size of the house like blizzard snow. Marcos often wondered how they found their front door.

James blinked, his face gaining that familiar shade of green. "Do people live here like this?" he exclaimed, bewildered.

"Yes." Marcos nodded gravely. "With little kids."

James huffed a sigh and shook his head.

"This is a hazard to us to get out." Marcos stared with dread at the yard, wondering what was in that package that would soon be added to their menagerie of toxic waste. "Anywhere you park or step, you are on junk or garbage. If you get out here, or anywhere like this, and are hurt or get sick from it, it's your fault." He gripped the steering wheel. "Watch the messages that come across the scanner in the mornings."

"Yeah," James acquiesced. "No kidding."

Marcos sighed, shaking his head. "It's a sad deal. I would love to help them, but they have to want to help themselves also. And at this time, they see nothing wrong with it."

James sucked in a lungful of breath, no doubt bracing himself for the landfill scent about to grace his sinuses. He slipped from the keep, clutching the package as if it were a parcel of great importance, and wandered through the maze. He got to the porch as quickly as he could, like he was running an obstacle course. His only opponent was the fact that he'd soon run out of breath and have to inhale. Having delivered the package, he shot back to the car, catapulting himself inside and slamming the door. Then, he released his breath and wrinkled his nose. "That is disgusting! How can people live like that?!" His chest caved in on itself as he heaved out a gag.

Marcos put the car in reverse and backed out as quickly as he could. "I don't know, but there are several around like this. But this is the worst one. You must keep your vehicle and yourself safe each day, so that you can complete the route." He angled back onto the road, glad to leave the

HAZMAT home behind. "I know that they told you to never take chances, and that is true. Some places out here, there is no cell phone signal and little traffic. If they are not watching our GPS closely, we could get in a bad spot and be there for a long time."

James shuddered. "That home *is* a bad spot."

Marcos didn't disagree.

Looking ahead at how much mail was left, James pulled a letter from the tote. Squinting at it, he took a few beats to try to decipher it himself before asking Marcos' opinion. "I have a letter here that says 'Granny,' but no address."

Oh, that. Marcos laughed, tossing a sideways glance at it. "I think it goes up here next. I saw that earlier, and guessed-o-mated that it goes there, but not sure." He smiled, shaking his head in fondness. "I always love Granny and Gramps' letters because many times, it's a guessing game. And I know that the sender wants to make contact. To most elderly people, that is love."

James clearly didn't share the same fondness for making people happy. "Why not just send it back?"

Affronted, Marcos held his breath a few moments before replying calmly. Maybe the kid didn't understand because he hadn't felt the sting of loneliness or fractured family. "Because these kids and grandkids are trying to make a connection, and we can either be stubborn or do the right thing, and make it connect." If he'd said it once, he said it a thousand times, and he was willing to repeat the same information. Not just to get it through James' thick skull, but because it was one of the most important things to him. "Like I said, for most of these people, we may be the only people they see most of the time. And if they have someone connecting with them, that can lift their spirit."

James fell quiet again, nodding quiet acquiescence. Marcos wasn't sure if he took the admonishment to heart and was letting his words sink in, or if he still felt like they should sever that connection. Marcos felt a twinge of concern, hoping that the residents of his small town would still get that much-coveted connection on his days off.

Another dreaded dirt road bridged the way between the next few houses to deliver. As Marcos bumped and bounced along, his tire sank into a pothole, then popped out again in teeth-jarring awareness. "Get good 8-ply or 10-ply tires on your vehicle so you get less flats," he stated the obvious. "And you *will* have flats."

James laughed. "Hey, I have roadside assistance. I'm not changing a flat."

Marcos fought the urge to grin. Maybe raise an eyebrow, adding an *oh, really* to the expression. *City boy.*

"I can call and wait on them," James finished off his proclamation with satisfaction.

Is that right? Marcos snickered. "Oh?"

"Yeah." James was all too proud of his precious roadside assistance.

"What are you going to do when you have no signal?" Marcos shrugged. Or, perhaps, the obvious one. "How far behind are you going to be when you wait on that roadside assistance for an hour or two?"

James' face darkened.

"Let me know how that works for you."

James shook his head, mumbled something.

"What was that?" Marcos couldn't hear over the future flats he was running over in the form of ill-maintained city roads.

"I don't know how to change a flat."

Well, that information didn't flabbergast him. Marcos sent a side glance at him and raised an eyebrow. "Really?"

James shook his head, bitterness dawning in his eyes.

"No one ever showed you how to change a tire?"

"No," James growled, turning a darkened glare to Marcos, as if he were offended that Marcos would insinuate that he was helpless. "There was never a need for it. My parents always had good tires. I don't remember them having a flat."

"You *will* get a flat." It was the Achilles heel of every driver, whether you drove a tractor, sedan, or anything in between. Shoot, even bikes had flats. "Look it up on YouTube. I bet there is a how-to change a tire on there."

James shrugged, "Okay," he replied in a tone that suggested he would do no such thing. Well, he could wait for his roadside assistance. Perhaps delivering mail at ten p.m. would be what it took for him to loosen a few lug nuts.

Eager to change the subject, James reached around into the back, withdrawing a package for an approaching house. Well, what was left of it. Along with the one Marcos had shoved in the mailbox yesterday, this one looked like it had been used to kick a few field goals, as well. Maybe had been run over by the previous mail delivery truck. "My goodness, this looks bad. It looks like someone drove over it."

Must have come from Shreveport. "Woo-hoo! That's a nice one." Marcos laughed. "I am glad she stamped it *damaged*." Otherwise, they may not have known!

James joined him in laughter, glad to be breaking the ice with a joke. "Damaged? That is *crushed*. Looks like it was spun out on as it got run over."

That was a good description. "Yeah, we get a lot of them like that." Marcos couldn't keep his laughter down. "That one is in pretty good shape compared to some. We have got them three years late and empty, but sometimes they are empty, but not too late."

James put the package back, his laughter returning in small bouts. "No way."

"Yep. Explaining that to people is difficult sometimes. Some people look at you like you are lying." Luckily, this one was going to a good house. Unlucky for the resident. "This lady will understand that we didn't do it, but if she calls, I'll say the new guy delivered it." He let his joke land, side-eyeing James, then laughed.

James returned his side-eye with a glare. "You're kidding, right?"

Marcos resorted to quieter snickering. "Maybe."

James rolled his eyes and simmered.

After delivering the poor, abused package, Marcos moved on to the next house. "Some people don't like me, or anyone else." He nodded to the next house on the list. "And that fellow there is one of them. He always has something negative to say. Me, being a nice fellow and praying for him. I see him in stores sometimes, and I start hollering his name, waving, asking how he is doing. He tends to duck and will usually reply reluctantly. He tends to look embarrassed. Not sure why." Marcos almost said something about heaping coals of fire on his head, but he was certain the teenage city boy wouldn't get that.

James steeled Marcos with a stare. "You really fit in here, you know that, right?"

Well, if that wasn't a compliment of the year. Marcos chuckled. "What, do you mean I'm a little touched as well?"

James kept up his poker face. "I'm not sure about a *little*, but you are definitely touched."

Marcos snickered. Then snickered, again. "Well," no retort came from his mouth. "You hang around here long enough, you will be, too."

He pulled up to another box, letting James take over the package for this one, since the car angled up the driveway. James pulled the lid down, freezing for a moment. "Is that a package?"

Marcos shot the mailbox a glance. "No, that is cardboard to keep the mail up. Close to the lid."

James did and hurled himself back into his seat. Marcos didn't put the car in drive, knowing there was more than just envelopes. How long would it take for his new trainee to notice, he wondered? "Some people don't like to reach far in their box to get mail and packages, but I always put the mail and packages close to the lid, except where we can't."

James nodded. "The mail I've seen in the boxes when I open them has been close to the lid as you said."

"Yep." Marcos prided himself on that. "But some people, they..." His voice trailed off. "Well, I'm not sure what they are thinking."

It was then that James noticed Marcos hadn't moved. It must've taken that to realize there was a package. He moved and pulled it from the back, like he intended to all along. "They have a package. What do I do with it?"

"Pull the cardboard out and put the package and mail in. That is a small box, and the package will fit, so no special treatment."

James nodded as he did what he was told.

"There are some special things we can do," Marcos finished. "But something if we did them after a while, we would have a hard time finishing on time."

Marcos pulled up to another mailbox, stuffing the mail inside. After checking the scanner, he put the car in drive and idled down the road. "This next house has nine packages."

James stiffened. Marcos heard a little clearing of his throat. "Okay." Marcos could only imagine what he was thinking. *What could those nine packages possibly be for?*

Who knew? "Make sure to put them in the pickup seat and close the door." He pulled into the driveway, pointing out the pickup in question.

"Sure." James stumbled out of the car, swinging the back door open. Marcos heard mutters between the rummaging of packages. Thankfully, they were a mixture, so the boy got good practice. Marcos watched as he stacked them against his chest and leaned backward, some type of balancing act as his skinny legs carried him toward the pickup. While he worked to open the door with the hand underneath the packages, Marcos grinned. Now seemed as good a time as any to grant one of James's wishes. A change of channel.

He switched the radio, turning the dial until some oldies but goodies shredded through the speakers. Ah, the 80s. Good times. Marcos grinned, sitting back. This should be fun to watch.

James finished delivering the packages and then returned to his car. As he stuffed himself inside the front seat, he paused, tilting his head as he stared at the radio. "Really?" He shut the door. "You go from Gospel music to Satan music. How do you manage that?" He paused, grinning. "I mean, that's Grandpa-music."

Now wait just a minute, here. "What? That's 80's rock!"

"Exactly."

Marcos shook his head, pulling out of the driveway. "You new generation-ers don't know what great music is because y'all had none." Well, James blew his chance at something different with comments like that. Grandpa-music. Right. "I tell you what. How about some Billy Graham?"

James visibly tensed, shaking his head. "No, no. I'm good with Grandpa Music!"

Oh, how quickly he back-pedaled. Marcos loved it. He switched the station until Billy Graham's passionate voice rang out, reading a passage of Scripture with eagerness. "No. This is better for you."

James sat stiffly, arms folded, as he glared a hole at his arch-nemesis, the radio. *I hate this,* the rods scribbled all over his face.

Marcos grinned. He moved on to the next house. "Okay. Get the mail and package for this next box in your hand, and ready before we get there."

James raised an eyebrow, but actually moved to do what he was told. "Okay?"

"That dog is vicious, and the box sits on the edge of the bank where the dog can climb in with us."

James' eyes widened. Well, Marcos had his attention now.

"Be ready to throw it in when I get to the box, because that mutt will be running down the hill."

James nodded. Marcos could almost hear the high-speed spy music playing upon approach. It felt like a spy operation, and if executed properly, hopefully they'd escape without any new bite marks to add to their menagerie of injuries, pride included. Only thing is, speed was the game, and James wasn't playing. He was still gathering the mail even as Marcos pulled up.

Come on, man. I'm going to get bit here.

Barking and teeth gnashing started down the hill. Nope. Too late. Marcos rolled up his window, easing forward. A hard *thud* drew James to look up with confusion. The dog's face appeared in the window, slobber dripping from his teeth as his snarls made it past. He bit at the window, growling and ferocious.

James jumped, scattering mail as he leaned back onto the console to get away from him. "What is the matter with that dog?" he demanded.

"Not sure." Marcos eased onto the road. "But it will bite. Never get out of here. It will end up injuring or killing someone. There are some bulldogs that are great and nice, and then there are the ones like that." Little growling devils, the lot of them. Marcos went up the road for about a half a mile. "Quick. Give me the mail."

James shoved it into his hand. Marcos eased his foot onto the gas pedal. Here we go...

The car idled forward. He rolled his window down. As they approached the mailbox, his blood pressure spiked. He slammed on his brakes just ahead of the barking dog, shoving the mail in the box. Not stopping to make sure it was all the way in, pressed the gas pedal, shooting off like a rocket. The dog's face reappeared, and his jaws snapped together, just under Marcos' arm. It was like some kind of scene from a movie.

He and James sat in silence for a few seconds as Marcos kept driving away from that mangy mongrel. "That dog needs to be put down before it hurts or kills someone." Marcos shook his head, determination in every shake.

Jame sat frozen in the seat. "Yeah. A lot of dogs on this route do."

Marcos turned around, breezing past that stupid dog, hearing its barks tailgating him up the road. By the time they reached the next box, they had both finally begun to breathe normally again. Marcos wished the box at the prior house had a mailbox as big as this one. But the bigger the box, the more mail stuffed inside, he thought. And not just the incoming mail, either.

He pulled around so James could reach it, watching to see his reaction. He wondered if James noticed the flag up, indicating some mail had to go out.

James opened the mailbox lid, and it came open like a wrecked car door under pressure. Inside, a wad of mail pushed against the lid. Some of it looked to have been there a while. James took some envelopes out, noticing a few with no postmarks. He sighed, reaching in and yanking out the stack. "Dude, is someone messing with this box?"

Marcos chuckled. "No. The ones that are open are the dad's letters. The ones going out are the kids' and the remaining is the mom's. Only take the ones without postmarks. This is not the only house where they have a lot of people living."

James muttered to himself, sifting through to find the ones with postmarks.

"A lot of time, I can blame crazy stuff like this on the new generation, but this is a multiple-generation thing. They just get what they want and leave the rest. People do strange things. I am sure that I do things that seem strange, too, and you do as well."

The comment landed, just as it was intended to. James' lip lifted in a sneer. "Well, I wouldn't do *that*." He nodded to the mailbox.

"Sure."

James handed back the mail accordingly, then stuffed the rest in the box.

Chapter 13

Marcos kept lightly bantering with his oh-so enthusiastic sidekick. With each passing mailbox, James lost a little more interest in his job. Marcos kept up the cheer, however. It wasn't his fault they were running late. Gravel under his tires, he hummed a little Gospel song so James would be sure to get a double dose of it – the music and the preaching – as the jeep bumbled along another familiar dirt road. Up ahead, Marcos spied something that quelled his humming. Despite the wide road, a full-sized truck had pulled off into the shoulder, emergency blinkers indicating that something wasn't right. Marcos slowed, calling out his open window to the driver, "Are you all right?"

A clean-shaven man somewhere up in his seventies peered out the window. Marcos recognized the truck as easily as he recognized the driver. Rufus. A man whose sense of humor was as dry as the dirt road he was stranded on. "Yes. I was talking to someone and lost signal. The signal isn't good today."

Glad that he was all right, Marcos chirped, "Yep. I usually get more calls, myself."

Rufus' glance darted up and down Marcos' jeep, disapproval slanting his eyes. "It looks like you've been running over some mailboxes with all those scratches."

Marcos snickered. Maybe not *quite* as dry as the dirt road. Just as pleasant to deal with, though. "Yeah, I was about to get yours in a few minutes." A wide grin spread across his face.

Rufus did no grin, as he found no humor in it. He leaned out the window, around Marcos, eyes settling on James. "Are you the new fellow?"

"Yes," James replies, hesitant.

Rufus swung his head in Marcos' direction. "Don't be running over mailboxes like he does." With that, he pressed the gas pedal, leaving them in a cloud of dust and poor jokes.

James blinked. "Well, he isn't very friendly."

"A little dry." Marcos was happy to be moving on. "But his wife has a sense of humor."

"Opposites attract, I guess." James shrugged.

For as late in the day and far into the route as they were, Second Street seemed like the wrong name for their street. A street with the name *second* should be early in their route, but it was not to be. But it was met with just as much trepidation, regardless. Marcos tensed as James perked up, remembering the fun from yesterday, gawking at girls.

"Which house is hers?"

"It's on the corner, there." Marcos fought the urge to roll his eyes. "Why? Do you know her?"

James grinned. "Not yet, but I will soon."

Was that a threat or a promise? Marcos took it as the former, but laughed nonetheless. "She is thirty-eight or thirty-nine years old. She is old enough to be your momma or grandma."

James snorted, wrinkling his nose. "No way," he said with disbelief.

"Yes." Marcos nodded, eagerly. Did James honestly think he knew more than the man who'd been delivering mail for 16 years? "I know her. She looks young, but she has kids older than you. I promise."

Regardless of her age, James looked ahead, eyes bolted on her house. "Is she married, or have a boyfriend?"

He was really not getting this, was he? "Not married, don't know about a boyfriend. I am telling you. I know her, and she would be mighty flattered, but she is almost 40."

They delivered her mail. James had stars in his eyes, the essence of puppy love as they drove off, even though she was nowhere to be found.

Disgusting.

Marcos left Second Street as quickly as he could, making their way down Oak. Next to the first box on the square, a gentleman stood, propping his arm up on it. Well, what do you know? Old David was out today. Although he certainly didn't look thrilled to be such.

Marcos' brakes squeaked as he eased to a stop. "Hey, there, David!"

David looked up and down the street, then leaned into Marcos' open window. "You're late."

Cheery. Sounded like a good day in the making. James' muscles tightened beside Marcos, ready for an onslaught of verbal abuse.

"I been here waiting for an hour. I'm expecting something important."

Weren't we all? "I'm training James here," Marcos nodded to the person in question. "As the relief carrier."

The explanation only caused David's eyes to narrow. "I don't care. There is no reason to be this late."

James didn't offer help or anything, just let his gaze flicker back and forth between speakers. That was fine. Marcos didn't want his feelings getting hurt as they had with Gene's. They were headed there next, so he figured he'd take this one for the team. "I'm sorry," Marcos apologized. "But we may be late tomorrow as well."

"If you are, I'll call the post master," David barked.

"Okay." Marcos handed him his mail, not worried about a thing. Let him call. He wasn't going to let David's foul mood ruin his. "I hope your day gets better." He made sure to add some extra cheer to his tone to irk David, who said nothing.

Marcos left the dark cloud behind. James didn't wait to get fully out of the driveway before asking with wide eyes his number one question:

"Is he always that way?"

"Yes," Marcos answered without thought. "But usually worse."

James stared at David hobbling back inside his house in the rearview mirror. "What does he get that is so important?"

"Nothing." Marcos plopped his shoulders in a shrug. "Mostly junk mail. Only thing that can help him is a prayer."

James sighed, shaking his head in doom and gloom. "What is the matter with people around here?"

"It's everywhere," Marcos said, sadly. "Not just here. Most people get mad about changes in their mail. There is never a dull day delivering mail."

"Clearly," James spat. He groaned as the houses counted down toward Gene's house. Marcos scanned the area, spotting Gene outside again today as he had been yesterday. Not wanting to rehash what had already happened, Marcos nodded to him. "He is out in the field on his side-by-side, but he is coming. So make it quick and get those packages scanned and run."

James didn't have to be told twice. He jumped from the keep like a secret agent, grabbed the packages, and ran toward the porch. Without waiting to see if Gene saw him, he sprinted toward the jeep again and threw himself inside. He slammed the door behind him.

Marcos began to pull away, then suddenly remembered. Or rather, *didn't* remember. He'd never heard the ding from the scanner. "You did scan them, right?"

James paused. Horror flushed his face, along with hot rage. "*No!*"

So much for not seeing him today.

Marcos stopped. James huffed a huge sigh. Marcos grabbed the scanner and handed it to him. It was his own fault, but he let it simmer.

Too late. The roar of a side-by-side filled the air, deafening them for a moment before Gene's face appeared by the window. He seemed to speed up as much as he could just to get to the car and cause trouble.

Marcos nodded out the window. "Run over there and scan them."

James shotgunned from the door again, running toward the house.

Marcos stepped out, smiling at Gene. "Good morning."

Gene's beady eyes were fastened on James as the side-by-side quieted to a lull. "What are you doing?"

"I sent him to double-check the scans," Marcos replied cheerfully, not wanting to throw James under the bus.

His only response was a grunt.

After taking the time to scan the packages, James returned to the car and climbed in. While he did, Marcos occupied Gene with as much conversation as he could. "Well, we'll see you tomorrow."

Before Gene could say anything more, he slipped back into the jeep and pulled away. Once they were on the road, Marcos glanced at James. James glanced over at him. Marcos just kept shaking his head, and shaking it the more he drove.

Marcos didn't speak again until they pulled up to a pedestal of four boxes. "You can tell they just put that one up." He pointed to the fourth box. Nicely painted, fresh numbers that were easily read. A postman's dream. "The lady at that mailbox? Her dad made the dad of the woman's box next to it mad when they were kids. And the one next to this one still hates her." What was it with these pedestal dramas? The last time they'd pulled up to a pedestal had many stories, too.

"Really?" James asked, deadpan, probably still mad about being sent back to scan Gene's boxes. Either that, or Marcos admonishing him for not doing it to begin with.

"Yes." Marcos nodded. "She told me last week that the new box messed up her spot to rest her feet, and it needed to be removed. I just listened to her and left it at that. There was no reason to argue." There wasn't a decent enough argument for that as it were.

"How old is she?"

"Seventy-something, I believe." Marcos finished with the mail, then began to drive off.

"Ah."

James didn't have much to say, and Marcos was as ready to get this day done as he could be. The next house had a small package, however. It seemed on the days they were running late, there were no shortage of packages.

James pulled up the scanner to scan the package, but frowned. "Hey, Marcos?"

"Hmm?" Marcos looked over.

James tilted the scanner to read what he narrated out loud. "It says to scan magazines, and then letters. How often does that actually happen?" He began scanning the necessary items.

"Sometimes once a week." Marcos shrugged. "Sometimes, a few times a week. Sometimes several times a day. Most of the time, it hits after you leave the box."

"Great," James mumbled.

"Yeah. The GPS isn't very accurate out here. Some places, it's off by miles, and some places, it's dead on. And others, it's off a few feet. If you get the mail in before it comes on, push the *passed already* option. Because if you pick some previous days' mail with today's mail, they throw a hissy fit. It may cause an uproar anyway, because a lot of time, part or all of outgoing mail goes to the wrong post offices and we don't get it till the next day or so."

"Makes sense," James said.

"The people with informed delivery used to get outraged when the mail that was supposed to show up for that day didn't show up, but now most realize the problem is getting it from the Shreveport distribution center to here. When they watch their packages bounce around this area sometimes for a month before it gets delivered, it makes sense to them as to why the mail is late."

James had been nodding for the past monologue, and when there was a break, he mumbled, "Can I scan the package now?"

"Yes." Marcos nodded.

James held the scanner to the package. A chirp filled the jeep, and he studied the screen before turning it to Marcos. Marcos read the message, alerting them that they were five miles away from the address they were currently sitting in front of. "What is that?" James huffed.

"Not sure." Marcos shook his head. "It's been that way since we got scanners. These eight houses in this stretch are all that way. Some of the others say a mile, some is just feet, like I was saying. The GPS is a problem, but I'm not sure if it's the only one." He grinned a toothy grin. "Well, look on the bright side. You won't deliver twenty packages a year down here."

James's bright side was an eclipse, and it showed in the way he sent Marcos a stare that seemed to say, *Oh, be quiet.*

Marcos didn't need the scanner for the rest of the route on the back road, nor did he need it to tell him what was coming next. He relied in part on the scanner and in part on his memory to tell him what packages went where. As he began to count down the last few houses of the day, he slowed to take a curve. "The house around the curve has a large package." He nodded to the sheet that James had pulled out after the scanner's wigging out. "This house is marked on your sheet. They are just grumpy about everything. There is no pleasing either of them. Typically, it is just the woman, but not in this case. I believe they have matching brooms."

James laughed at the reference from earlier.

"But." Marcos had to find that silver lining, somewhere. "She rocks that 80s hairdo every day." Perfect to match the music they'd been listening to, briefly.

James waited until the jeep pulled to a stop to get out. He wrestled the huge package from the back and found his balance before he started toward the house. The owner appeared at the door, sixty years of life creasing her face. James handed the package off to her and exchanged a few words. Marcos observed him shake his head and give her a polite smile as he headed back. As he got in, he sent Marcos a wary look. "She was real nice. Offered me tea. And I've never seen hair like that, except in old movies."

Old? Feeling suddenly ancient, Marcos raised an eyebrow. "Watch it! The 80s weren't that long ago." Well, glad that she was nice to him. Beginner's luck. Marcos began to pull away. "And just wait. You will see the real person soon."

Marcos turned back onto the main road and pulled over to the box. James frowned, confused. "The flag isn't up."

One out of many. "Check it, because they are bad about putting mail in the box and not raising the flag. And if we don't get mail that day, they call the post master complaining, and then he calls me, mad." Hadn't he told that story before? The postmaster's endless complaints he received? He was doing everything he could to avoid another one of those conversations.

Affronted, James did as he was told. "Man, people around here are grumpy."

Well, his impression of the 80s hairstyle and her invitation to tea had worn off quickly. "People are just picky about how their mail is handled. Or if it's late. These people wake up in misery."

James snorted a laugh of agreement.

"We don't have anything for this next house," Marcos nodded to the next house on the route. "But if you have a package, he will come out in just an adult diaper, and his wife will come out in a thin nightgown. And you are going to want to be in a hurry, there."

James's face crunched just as it had when he'd eaten those bug cookies yesterday. "That is disgusting."

"Well, they don't really get any company." Marcos shrugged it off. "You will notice the women that stay home, when they get packages, will have nearly nothing on for the most part. But some will be thoroughly dressed. Just be extra nice because you will find out if they come out to get the package. You can get through faster, typically. Personally, I don't care what they do or don't wear if they come out to get their stuff."

He was sure James didn't share the same nonchalance as he did. So long as it wasn't Synthia or one of the girls he had been gawking at earlier.

Marcos slowed on the dirt road, hitting the washboard-style the city was known for. He sighed, shaking his head. "You will have to get used to these dirt roads, but it shouldn't take long."

For a country boy, maybe. He wasn't sure about the city boy. Just ahead, at the next mailbox, Marcos noticed two things: That the box had mail inside, and a fellow was walking up to the jeep as it approached. Speaking of prison, Marcos silently remarked. He kept Jimmy's history to himself, not wanting James to change his attitude upon knowing Jimmy's skeletons in his closet. Jimmy'd had his fair share of being in prison at different times for different reasons. But it seemed as though today was one of his better days as he clutched his Bible down at his side. It didn't stop Marcos from rolling down the window and smiling out at the man. "Hey, Jimmy, how's it going?"

"It's a great day." Jimmy smiled and leaned down to see Marcos better. "Can you, by chance, call my aunt for me? My phone isn't working, and my truck isn't either."

"Sure." Marcos put the jeep in park. He fished his phone out of his pocket, typing in the number as Jimmy dictated. Hearing the chirping rings in his ear, Marcos handed the phone off to Jimmy and let him talk to her.

"'Yello!" Jimmy said to his aunt on the other line.

"This should take a second," Marcos said to James as he delivered the mail. They waited for a few moments as Jimmy finished filling his aunt in on everything and hung up, handing the phone back to Marcos. Tempted to grab it with some hand sanitizer, Marcos took it back. "Thanks, man," Jimmy said to him.

"Sure thing." Marcos put the cell phone away. "Have you been doing good?"

"Yes." Jimmy smiled. "I'm doing good. God has treated me good."

It was amazing how a person's life could change. Marcos returned his smile. "That's great! Are you still going to church?"

"Yes." Jimmy nodded with enthusiasm. "The preacher comes and picks me up."

"Well, that's great." Marcos tapped the side of the jeep. "I hope you keep doing good."

"I plan to," Jimmy assured him with a quiet smile. "See ya later."

"You, too, man." Marcos quipped cheerfully, then pulled away. Once they were out of earshot, James gawked at him. "I can't believe you let him use your phone."

"That is what I should have done," Marcos answered. "And that is what God would have wanted me to do." He didn't miss James' eye roll. "I have worked on Jimmy a few times, trying to keep him alive, and he has really changed. He is suspected of killing a few people."

James gave a start. He stared at Marcos with wide eyes, his expression ever changing deeper and deeper with horror.

"I am sure whoever killed them had a reason, because they were all into drugs," Marcos made his opinion clear without saying it. "He has always been nice to me. Even if he hadn't been, I would have let him use my phone. Besides." He grinned at James. "No sense in making a murderer mad!"

James swallowed and glared at Marcos. "Very funny." He eyed the house, no doubt memorizing which one housed a potential murderer. Marcos hoped he wouldn't be unkind after this.

A few houses down, they pulled up to an older mailbox, one of the larger ones. James eased to the side to put the mail in it as Marcos angled so he could reach it. The mailbox swung, hanging on for dear life as James tried to do his job. James struggled to get the lid up. "Man, that has a heavy lid."

"It has never been fastened all these years I've been doing this." Marcos chuckled.

"No way." James tried to close it, despite the fact that it wouldn't seal.

"Wiggle it," Marcos tried.

James gently tugged it, but even with the gentle motion, the mailbox shifted over by a few inches. But the mail was sealed inside. James splayed his fingers, carefully removing his hand as if handling a bomb, and eased back inside. "How does it sit there like that?"

Marcos pulled away with just enough caution. "It's heavy. And evidently, the board under the box lid is smooth. I have seen it blown off in a couple of storms, but that is it."

"I can't imagine it not falling over," James said, settling back.

Marcos didn't bother accelerating as the next house was right next to the swinging mailbox. "This next house is a hard one to figure out. People move in and out like fleas, and we never know exactly who lives there, because most of these people don't put forwards in. My telepathy and guessing isn't very good at figuring out who lives there."

James snickered, probably figuring out by now that some postal customers expected him and Marcos to be mind readers. "Don't worry." Marcos grinned, referencing James' first day on the job. "Some are scribblers, but that is usually how we know who moved in or out. There are several around here like that."

"Sounds like fun," James said, sarcastically.

Marcos finished with the route on this road. That was it. Slowly counting down the remainder of roads until they could take the one back to the post office. But that didn't mean that they had to rush through it. "Watch out on this road. People are set in their ways, and drive like they are on fire."

James nodded as the sounds of an engine revving caught both their attention. Marcos swung a look in the rear-view mirror and shrugged, pulling over to a mailbox. The truck behind him, which had been tailgating, flew around him, nearly losing control as he left Marcos in the dust, taking off like a jet.

"Just like that one."

James laughed, staring out the window. Marcos pulled away. As they made their way down the street, they passed a sign that read, *slow, children at play.* It brought back memories of the day before, when the girl had wrecked her car. Hadn't there been a similar sign out there, as well?

"You are right about those signs."

"Yep." Marcos chuckled. "And if there was a kid at play, it better be fast."

James did a double-take. "That's just wrong."

"Well, you've seen how fast that truck was going." Marcos nodded to the maniac race car driver disappearing down the road. "That's normal. And they drive in the middle of the road."

"I can see that." James glared out the window.

Marcos continued counting down the houses in his mind, and along with them, the amount of packages he had to deliver. Most of them were on the larger scale, he noticed. Needing someone to spill his thoughts to – teenager or otherwise, he released his thoughts. "Most of these boxes are small, and there are a lot of people that get big packages nearly every day. You would think they would put up a bigger mailbox, but no. Unlike the parcel companies, we have to do the mail *and* packages, and a number of these boxes makes it take a lot longer to get finished, especially on heavy mail volume days."

"I am catching on to that," James admitted bitterly, casting a glance at the time.

"People are funny about their mail." Marcos shook his head. "There is no explanation for it."

As if his statement needed evidence to support it. He stopped, pulling up to a mailbox near a house. Too near, as James pointed out.

"This box is literally 30 feet from the front door with a lock on it. Why?" he demanded.

"Well, it's called *paranoia*." Marcos released a breath as he shook his head. "I can't explain it. Look at the houses and yards that have these, because they all resemble each other. Luckily, this one only gets mail half the time and only a few packages."

James still sighed. "The lock box looks more expensive than their car."

Kid was sharp. Smarter than the homeowners, at this rate. "Yep." Marcos let James deliver the mail, fiddling with the lock, then drove off, leaving the house of paranoia behind. He turned up the road, where some newer mailboxes aligned the shoulder, standing tall and proud, and not whittled away with rust and loose lids. There was a story behind that, as there was a story behind every mailbox. "Here, a while back, someone drove right up this road, knocking boxes off with a bat or something." He pointed to the fairly new mailboxes aligned along the road. "They stopped at this box." He eased up to the box in question, a large mailbox that looked to be regular on the surface.

"I noticed all the others were new," James commented. Funny what you could see when you weren't gawking at girls. Maybe the kid did have some observance after all! "Why did they stop here?"

Marcos grinned as he eased up to the mailbox. "Open it."

James reached for the lid, and surprise tightened his muscles. "Dang! That's heavy!" He grunted, letting the lid fall. "And thick." He blinked, realizing why it was so heavy. "And... on a steel pipe."

Marcos laughed. "I would have loved to have been watching when they hit that box. I believe they were sore."

James nodded, ever so slowly. "I can see why this was the last box they hit."

Marcos chuckled as he pulled away. "By the way. You are going to scrape boxes and limbs, so put a magnet on the side to protect your door. The lids will pop down while you're moving. Sometimes, the box will fall on the door when you pull the lid and so on."

James snorted, wrinkling his nose and craning his neck backward in determination. "I won't be scraping any boxes."

So he was a better driver than Marcos, a 16-year mail-carrier veteran, eh? He chuckled. "Okay." No sense in arguing that one. "Go by the main post office before you come in tomorrow and look at the vehicles there."

James huffed another sigh. Marcos wasn't sure if he was willing to be as humbled as all that, but it was worth a try.

The afternoon grew later, but they were still making up for lost time. Marcos pulled up to the next box, noting the flag was up. He angled the jeep so James could reach inside.

James must've expected some outgoing mail or something, from the way his head bounced back as he peered inside. "It's something in aluminum foil." He reached inside, drawing out the object. "With a note."

Marcos glanced over, scanning the note. "Aww. He made you a special brownie."

James eyed Marcos, with uncertain wariness in his gaze. After his experiences with food, he wasn't about to go trying to eat anything else. He'd said as much to Marcos.

"He makes a lot of Super Brownies for people around here," Marcos explained, most helpfully.

"Are they good?" James asked with a hint of distrust. Probably wanted to eat something, but after being traumatized twice, he wasn't about to take that first bite without running it through a lab, first. And seeing as how there was no lab on the run, Marcos would have to do.

Not that he was very good at test results. "I hear he is a great cook."

James' mouth practically watered as he looked down at the brownie again.

"But you can't eat it."

Disappointment deflated James's posture.

"But you have to take it and leave this thank you note."

James didn't look too thrilled about taking some extra time to thank the man for something he couldn't eat. With a slight pout to his lip, he combined his *thank-you* note with the man's mail and left it behind. He settled back into his seat, reminding Marcos of a little kid who didn't get his way. "It smells great. Why can't I eat it?"

Marcos had even said *special. Special* brownie. What did James think that meant, that it had candy in it? "It's a super-brownie. With a kick. Not a regular one."

James' confusion only deepened. Did Marcos really have to spell it out for him? That these were the types of brownies places like Colorado or California were famous for?

"It has a special additive," Marcos tried one more time.

"Huh?"

Marcos felt like surrendering. "Do I have to draw a map?"

A map? He could see the words written across James' face. "What?"

Oh, come on! "You won't pass a drug test."

James paused. For too long, he paused. Thought. Pondered. Then, his eyebrows lifted. "Ohh."

"Yeah." Marcos blinked and returned his eyes to the road.

Chapter 14

Not much farther, now. Marcos was eager to get home to his wife and clock out from this babysitting job. You can't tell him that James didn't know what special brownies were...

Choosing to drop the topic, he changed the subject and pointed to a yellow-trimmed home with a mailbox nicely tucked at the end of their driveway. The mailbox was the size of a small shoe, but at least it was well-marked. "This house here gets lots of packages. And, of course, they have the small box. They are not going to be happy if we leave a package or take it to the post office. Most of the time, you can't get out for the dogs. When you can leave it, they won't like where you put it, so the dog doesn't get it."

"These people." James attempted to shove the package into the mailbox.

"Always be nice. It won't help, here, but maybe one day it will."

James slammed the lid. "Are they old?"

"No." Marcos eased back onto the road. "Maybe 30ish. Just miserable."

"Like everyone else around here."

Marcos nodded, marking off two more houses before easing to a stop in front of another one. "This house here? They tend to be part of scams, like credit card fraud, using all kinds of names. One time, they got one in the post master's name. He didn't appreciate it."

James smiled, faintly. "How do you know it was in his name?"

"The spelling was exact, and his name is spelled differently than any others around here with the same first name."

"Ah."

"Yes, he was less than amused." Clearly the opposite of Marcos, who released a small chuckle to convey his amusement.

"What happened?" James asked, eagerly.

"Nothing." Marcos shrugged. "The postal inspectors said they didn't want to mess with it, and the people at the address promised not to do it anymore. They forgot about that real quick."

"Well, that's disappointing," James said. "I was hoping for a good story."

"Oh, I have plenty of those." Marcos laughed, pulling up to the next house. "Take this one, for example. They are all on SSI and Food stamps, and you will get blamed every time something is late. There are three generations there. They will work for cash. They smoke, drink, and do all kinds of other drugs and have bulldogs. No, you do not get out there under any circumstance."

"I'm starting to see more and more of that. I'm good with it." James' tone lilted, happy at the thought of having fewer houses he'd have to exit the vehicle for.

Marcos pulled to the mailbox, letting James deliver the mail next. He took one look at the house and snickered. "Do you need a cat or dog?"

"No, I'm good." James shook his head.

"Well," Marcos looked back at the house. If it could be called that. *Pound* might be a better word. "This next house is the cat lady's house. She also has dogs outside in kennels. She tries to rescue animals, mainly cats. I think she means well, she is real nice. Your stomach will hurt from the stench if you go up there or get close."

James gagged at the thought.

"She doesn't realize it. Be nice to her, though. Most people are not." Probably why she collected as many animals as she could. At least they appreciated her and her efforts. "You won't see her very often. She could set you up with a cat or dog."

"I think I'm good," James eyed the yard warily and shook his head. "I have enough to worry about taking care of."

Marcos left the cat lady behind, easing to a stop in front of a widow's house. He didn't see her out in her yard today, but perhaps James would get to meet her sometime. "This next box is a sweet elderly widow. A few months ago, her husband passed away."

James sobered, accordingly. "That's sad."

"He was a good man as well. Well, she was getting letters for him after he passed, and I guess one day, she had had enough. I went by a couple of weeks ago. The flag was up, and a handful of mail was there with notes written on each one that said, *no longer lives here. He now resides at Ash Cemetery; not sure the address.*" Despite the situation, he found himself snickering as he shook his head. "I laughed so hard. She has a sense of humor."

James matched his laughter. He leaned his head against the seat, staring at the headliner as he did. "Oh, that was good."

"They never came back!" Marcos chirped. "So I didn't have to attempt them." He watched to make sure that James had at least learned the word for *attempting* to deliver the mail the first time during his training.

He didn't balk at it, so he probably had. "I probably wouldn't, either." James chuckled. "Come back, that is."

They fell into a comfortable silence. Marcos had stories, oh, he had stories for each house they delivered to, but he didn't want to overload James with an entire five-volume series of personal experience, so he saved a few for tomorrow. He'd need them if the day was anything like it was today. He'd need something to pass the time as they got down to the last few houses.

"How do you know where you're going?" James surprised him by breaking the silence. "Learning the route, and stuff."

"Most of it comes from doing it for 16 years," Marcos replied. "That being said, don't trust your phone's GPS because it's likely to take you to the wrong house. It could take you to a lake." Marcos wouldn't have minded if he hadn't been running late the day the GPS took him to the overlook. "It might take you to the right house as well. Use it with caution, and you can call me if you need to." He ended with an evil laugh. "I typically don't bite people on the first call."

He was surprised that James took the bait for another joke. "So I'll have to use that phone call sparingly, then." His grin matched Marcos'. He wasn't sure if James was lightening up because they were getting closer to the end of the day, or if he enjoyed banter more when he wasn't pouting about something. Seemed like a good kid. Just flirtatious and very green.

Happy to have found an easy conversation between them, Marcos settled into the seat as he drove at a leisurely pace, stopping periodically at each house and lightening the load of mail with each one. "The previous mail clerk at this office knew all the scoop. She listened to everyone's gossip and would usually get all sides. I mean," Marcos plateaued his hand across his chest. "She was chest deep into it." He could picture the previous clerk and how everything took twice as long with her. "Did you see how fast Lizzy put the letters in the boxes?" James nodded. "Yeah, it was like lightning."

"Not the previous one." Marcos glanced in his mirror. "She would look at each letter slowly and hold it up to the light if necessary. Sometimes she would say, 'I wonder what is going on with them,' and a few days later, she would tell me about it. She was good at extracting information. She would act like a concerned Grandma!"

James blinked in surprise. "How did she do that and get by?" Not something that would fly in Little Rock, for sure.

"Everyone knew how she was, and most didn't mind. Also it's a small office, so she could take her time."

"But makes us late!" James pointed out. "I'm glad we have Lizzy, now, and not that other girl."

"Me, too." Marcos eased to a stop in a house. Like all the others, chalk-full of memories. Some of which he would enjoy forgetting. "I came up with a signature confirmation to this address the other day, and no one answered the door. So, I went on down the road. After I finished, I turned around. When I came back, the girl was standing by the mail box in a towel, with another towel around her hair. And it was *dusty*." Marcos yielded to laughter. "She wanted that package."

"How old?" James asked with perhaps a little too much hope. Marcos silently berated himself for telling that story to the kid who gawked at anyone under forty, and even the forty-year-old ones, too.

"Eighteen."

James paused too long. Irritatingly long. "What does she look like?"

It was Marcos' turn to roll his eyes, clearly in competition with James for how many eye-rolls they could give in a day. "You can girl shop after hours."

Affronted, James huffed a sigh. Before he could berate Marcos for calling it what it was, *girl shopping*, Marcos cut off any further talk about it. He pulled up to a mailbox, one that had recently complained over an issue that everyone hated. Might as well point it out to James, so he could hate it, too. "The most despised piece of mail you will deliver, even above junk mail, is water bills. They really suck and stick together. People always get mad every month because some will be stuck together. I have never heard of a mail carrier who liked them. If someone said they do, they are lying."

"I heard people at Little Rock talking about them," James said in an *aha* tone. "I didn't understand why."

Marcos laughed. "You will find out in a few days, and will be reminded each month. Because I will be taking off those days."

James glared, jutting his chin out and shaking his head. "Very funny."

Oh. He thought Marcos was joking.

James pulled out the next round of mail, but paused, doing a double-take at the envelope facing upward at him. "Hey. This postmark is from last year."

"Yeah," Marcos snorted a laugh. "It happens a lot. The water bills from the town started coming in later and later, after they were sent to Shreveport for processing, which makes no sense to start with. They should have been received here, and the carrier given credit for delivering them and taken out. But logic don't happen in the postal service. You have people in offices that don't live in reality." Sometimes he wondered if it was like stepping through an office door erased all logic. Whatever the case, they seemed to forget what it was like to live in the everyday world. "Anyway, one month, they didn't show up at all for the whole town. The next month, they sent the bills out and those came trickling in over a weeks time and then a week or so later a tray with the previous months bills came in, all of them. You know they were in a closet somewhere in Shreveport."

"I bet a lot of people were mad over the late fees," James remarked.

Marcos tsked. "You bet it." He stopped at another one. Getting closer to the end, now. He couldn't wait. "We get mail, both bills and junk that are labeled, 'unable to forward,' even though they are good addresses. We have pulled labels off 2 trays of mail before, like, 2,000 letters there about. It was just to keep people from around here getting mad. And," he rubbed his fingertips together, easing away the memory. "That cuts your fingers. The labels are sharp. The REA bills come in long trays, and one month, we had not gotten any. Then, just a few days before the bills were due, an REA truck pulls up outside the post office and brings the bills in. They had been sent off as normal, but returned to the mail office all labeled, *unable to forward*. That made the news." Marcos chuckled as he shook his head, remembering that chaotic moment when he'd given up on ever going home for that day with the increase in mail.

"That is hard to believe." James shook his head in that same disbelief. "We don't seem to have that problem where we live."

"Your mail comes from Little Rock," Marcos explained, slightly envious. "Nowhere near as bad as Shreveport. They don't care."

"Apparently." James handed over the next stack of letters.

As soon as Marcos delivered them, his lips curved in a smile. "I'll tell you another good one. In 2020, 2021, while COVID-19 was pressing on, people were not getting their mail and packages. People working there in Shreveport Distribution Center were taking all their sick leave, as they had extra. Well, one day, a local TV station stuck a camera up outside the complex. And lo, and behold, there were tents filled with packages under them, and trailers filled with mail and packages. People were *angry*."

James emphasized his head shakes with bewilderment. "What did they do?"

Do? That would imply taking action, right? Marcos released a small laugh. "They got clerks from all over including up here that would volunteer to go help sort them out and get packages sent out. They paid them mileage, too. Well, it wasn't long before the postmasters stopped sending them because, from the ones I talked to, they would be working and the employees from the Shreveport Distribution center would watch them. Real peaches down there."

"Peaches, huh?" James snorted. "Sounds like it."

"Indeed, it – " Marcos spotted the long stripe lying across the road and stiffened. It wasn't just a stripe; it was a living, breathing reptile he did not want in his undercarriage. Forgetting the talk about Shreveport, he yanked his steering wheel to the right. The jeep followed suit, shaking its occupants to the right, then back to the left again. He didn't miss it, however. A little *bump* under the jeep sent him and James up and down before the jeep continued on like nothing happened.

James' eyes were wide, fastened out the windshield as he relived the moment mentally. Not only that, he began to fold himself into the seat, scrunching his knees against his chest. "That's a big snake."

Wow. Marcos had never heard his voice so high-pitched. He put the jeep in reverse and began to back up, eyeing out the rear windshield for that snake. James fumbled for the window switch and began frantically rolling up his window.

"It was a rattler," Marcos stated for the record.

James didn't care. He cared more about getting farther away from the snake, not closer to it. "What are you doing!?"

"Backing up to check on it," Marcos replied calmly.

James swallowed. Breathless, he looked backward. "It's fine! I see it moving."

Guess he didn't like snakes either, huh? "I am just trying to get an up-close and personal view."

"I don't need one!" James howled.

Marcos eased his brakes. Stopped in the middle of the road, a few feet away from the snake. "Well, I guess it's gone."

"That's great!" The relief on James' face was palpable. "Let's go. We've got mail to deliver."

Marcos never knew him to be so eager to do his job. Delighted with his little prank, he put the jeep in drive, leaving the portion where the snake was in a cloud of dust. Sometimes it was fun to mess with his little prodigy.

Turning onto the main highway, Marcos let the dust settle from the incident with the snake – literally – before trying to talk to James, again. He wasn't sure if it was a good time to follow such a prank with a story more harrowing in nature, but he couldn't exactly let it go, either. The memory was one that burned in the front of his mind, rather than the back. "I was headed hunting early one morning, and right up that hill along the side of the road, I saw a hand raise up. It was right at daybreak."

James lowered his feet to the floorboard, but stopped before they hit. His eyes went wide as he waited for Marcos to finish the rest of his story.

"I thought I was seeing things at first, but I turned around, and it was a woman all broken up and hurt. She had flown off the road in the middle of the night and went way down the hill. She spent the rest of the night climbing an inch at a time out of there."

James swallowed. "Did she live?"

"I don't know." Marcos shook his head. "Never heard anything. She was bad off."

He could still see it. The sun resting on the horizon, shining some beams upon the world with promise of a beautiful day. Then, that. A broken hand, a woman's face painted in bruises and caked with dried blood. And that look in her eyes... that wild, crazed look that screamed out *help me* at the same time, trying to process what she'd been through. Marcos truly hoped she made it. He'd never heard much after that about her, but the woman hadn't given up. She'd survived, an inch at a time, and made it to the road. Marcos hoped that same survival had carried her through to healing on the other side.

He glanced over at James, who couldn't even change a tire and let a sigh inflate his lungs. "I know you are young, now. But look ahead at your future. Manage your health, help others, and let God be in charge. And you will have a good life even through the bad times."

James fell silent. Marcos hoped his thoughts were at least louder than his quietude.

***

James couldn't shake it. One moment, Marcos was halfway through a humorous tale about something that had happened to him during his time as a mail carrier. The next, he wandered through the haunted graveyard of his memories, laid to rest there. James expected he probably saw a lot, both as a mail carrier and as a first responder.

He just wished Marcos would stop preaching at him.

He always brought up God, as if he hadn't even heard that James didn't follow Him. Between that, the constant praying, and the Gospel music, James felt like the front seat of the jeep was one of those church pews he used to sit in. He'd seemed to understand that James avoided religion like the plague, but still kept bringing his into it.

Yet something in his somber tone tempted him to take it seriously. But James was determined not to end up like these people here. It was obvious they needed prayer – and James wasn't the praying type. But he was fine. He would be fine. He was eighteen, he had a job, at least for the moment, if he decided to come back.

Today hadn't been as bad as the first two days, but it was long, boring and it stretched on forever. The people were awful. Marcos was way too happy and there were too many boxes. Maybe he should find something closer to home.

Or, maybe, he should stick this one out. Maybe it would get better. He hoped so. Because he knew, as of right now, he wasn't entirely happy with the new job. It was, to say the least, overwhelming.

Chapter 15

Shaking off the memory of that harrowing morning when he'd spotted the woman by the side of the road, Marcos pulled up to one of the last houses on the routes. "For this next house, you have a big package. When you get out, put it on the chair by the door and be quick. The wife here is mad because no one was home the other day to sign for a package, so I took it back to the post office. Just be nice and quick."

"How is that your fault?" James crunched his face. "They weren't home!"

"She thinks it is." Marcos shrugged it off. Some people just needed someone to blame for their personal woes and misery. Might as well be the mailman. "Her husband, he don't care. But she will be mad for a while." Marcos pulled in the rest of the way, sighing with relief. "I think they're gone."

James wasted no time sprinting out of the jeep. Making sure to scan it, he nestled it where Marcos instructed in the seat of the rocking chair, then sprang back to the jeep. He closed himself inside. Marcos didn't wait to pull out of the driveway.

He was about to drive past the next mailbox, having no mail for it, but his eyes caught the flag sticking up. He eased to a stop and James rolled down his window, still sealed shut from that snake incident. Once it was rolled down far enough, he reached inside. Marcos saw him deflate, having run into another problem with outgoing mail. "It has a stack of mail that says, 'doesn't live here.'"

Oh, great. More scribblers. Just what they wanted when they were down to thirty more houses until they could go home. "Let me see it."

James removed the stack and shoved it at Marcos. He started thumbing through it. "Oh, that's her brother, that's her sister, that's her brother-in-law," he mumbled each relation as he looked through it, ending with a laugh. "I guess she don't want the electric bill anymore. It's in his name." Still, with a shrug, Marcos handed the stack back to James. "Put them in a rubber band, and we will make a note of the names and return everything for them. She does this every so often. They live with her for a while, and then she runs them off. She uses them to pay the bills and food. She is a real jewel." Nice and sweetly sarcastic, there. "She will come up to the post office in a few days, mad that we are sending everything, including the bills, back for these names. That is what she does."

"Great. I look forward to that." James snapped the rubber band around the stack of mail, enough to warrant the cutting down of at least one tree, and secured them with the other outgoing mail.

Marcos eased up to the next one. "There are a lot of duplicate and triplet numbers, like 385 here. There are four roads with that number. There are seven roads with the number 105, and two roads with the number 460." Might as well get the confusion out of the way now. "Not only that, but there is also one number, with several boxes like A,B,C or 1,2,3. So, you really have to pay attention to the roads. Some of these road names are something else, like Bunny Hop."

He noticed James stiffen, his face clouding over. "So, I can't really go by name or number, but by road with number." He swallowed. "That will be hard to sort."

Doing one's job could be difficult, couldn't it? Slowing down and paying attention to the road names along with the numbers, not just the numbers, imagine that! Marcos bit back his insults, returning to his mantra from Monday. *Vacation. Vacation. Vacation. Tropical beach,* yeah right, *road trip. Time off.* He chose to be politically correct this time, though he had to grit his teeth all the way through it. "Well, it's not too bad. It will take some work, but you can do it."

Leaving no room for argument, he eased to a stop at the end of the road. Well-practiced in driving, he threw a look in the mirror, frowning at what he saw. *Is that the same truck?*

A logger truck started as a speck in his mirror, but gradually grew to a full-size vehicle, barreling down the road. *I'll be darned, it is the same one.*

Marcos recognized the hood ornament on the same grille that had flattened that poor stop sign earlier today. The truck rode up on his tailgate enough for him to catch a glimpse of the logo painted on the side of his door to confirm.

Marcos hurried to the side of the road, getting into the shoulder earlier than he normally did. He was not going to be the next object this logger truck cut down.

Rather than slowing down and waiting for him to finish delivering the mail, the logger truck swerved to the left, laying on its horn for a moment enough to make James jump. Marcos hummed a little song to himself as he busied himself with the mail delivery, while the truck snaked by them. Once the logger truck had passed them, he drifted over onto his side of the road again. Marcos was surprised that he remembered to get back over. The logs in the back of the cradle bounced, as if waving at him, screaming for help. He couldn't help but chuckle to himself at the red flag attached to one of the logs that waved in the wind.

You got that right. That truck is *a red flag.*

By now, James' pleasant banter had dissolved behind a cloud of his poor mood, or rather, his discouragement. Marcos wasn't sure which was which anymore. Still, he couldn't keep this good of a story to himself.

Marcos eased back onto the road. "I don't know if you noticed the stop sign on the ground by the post office, but the fellow that drives that truck that just passed us ran over it this morning, and drove on like nothing happened."

A laugh burst from James' lips, however halfhearted. "Are you serious?"

"Yep." Marcos grinned at the memory. "He lives a block from there."

"That's crazy," James replied. "Can't he get in trouble for that?"

"Not around here. They will put it back up sometime." Marcos waited for his turn in traffic, then eased out onto the road. "He took off from the store where we stopped earlier with the fuel hose stuck in his gas tank. He did return it, but it was worn down, some." He chuckled a little bit. "I don't think he should be driving."

"Yeah, how did he ever get his license?" James laughed. "A fuel hose, really?"

"Yep." Marcos chuckled, pausing in front of another house. "Okay, so this next box?"

James looked out the window.

"It's a married couple, but the wife has a P.O. Box where she gets credit card statements and a bank statement, and her husband doesn't know about it, and we don't tell."

"Really?" Curiosity sparked in James' eyes.

"We have to pay attention, because some of them come to her mailbox, so we have to hand it to Lizzy."

"People are weird around here." James shook his head. Another one of his favorite phrases.

Marcos hadn't given much thought to how many stories he was made aware of until he started telling James as they passed each house. He turned up a dead-end road. Marcos pointed to a house on the right, near the corner, to James. "There used to be an old man, like a real hillbilly, living in that house there."

If it could be called a house. More like a shed, really. "It is small, like a tiny house. But nice for out here in comparison to these others." James shrugged. "Heck, the yard isn't full of junk." His tone sounded far too happy for such a statement.

Marcos exhaled, something that might be considered a laugh, or perhaps an acknowledgment. "Yep. That is because he is dead, now."

Well, that soured the mood. "Oh."

"The previous carrier before me didn't see him for a few days, and the mail wasn't getting picked up, so she told the one neighbor that he associated with. He went down there and found him face down in a bowl of cereal. He was evidently very well on his way to decomposing."

James' face scoured, and he let a little gag loose. "That is awful. Did he not have any family?"

"Yep," Marcos clipped. "He did. They were waiting him out so they could sell what he had."

"I doubt they got much," James remarked bitterly.

"Oh," Marcos raised his eyebrows. "But it was. He squired everything away, and his property sold very high after they cleaned it up. Not counting what they got for the metal."

"I see," James remarked.

Marcos pulled up to the next house. The roof slanted forward, revealing about a dozen or so buzzards sunning themselves on the roof. "Hey. Look at the roof."

James leaned around him, surprise twitching his gaze. "There are buzzards all over it! And in the dead tree by it."

Marcos nodded, eyeing the carrions with suspicion. "Last week, I got a little extra concerned because he wasn't getting the mail out of his box. He has had buzzards up there for a long time, but they got worse recently. So after talking with Lizzy, she called a friend of hers that is a county cop and told him. He went right there. She was on the phone with him when he started up the driveway and saw them on the chimney. He said, 'Oh no.' He just knew by looking that the man was dead inside, probably in front of the fireplace."

Engrossed in the story, James nodded.

"He hung up and called her back a half hour later. He told her he beat on the doors for ten minutes, and finally the man opened the door, surprised that he was there but thankful someone was concerned."

"I just knew he was going to be rotten," James exclaimed in wonder.

"Not this time." Marcos checked the gauges on the dashboard, noticing one of the tires was low. Not enough to be concerned, he'd checked them that morning. But still, he pointed it out. "You need to keep a check on vehicle fluids, lights, tires, brakes and so on. I have had the brakes go out on me more than once on a newer vehicle, partly from being on the brakes all day, but also from things in the road. Make sure you check your vehicle in the mornings to make sure lights and stuff are working properly, like they told you to."

James glanced at the dash. "Got it."

Marcos took the road at a slower pace, his eyes drifting over toward the street crossed by the one they were on. His instinct told him that his little talk about using the brakes was going to come in handy. A car idled up to the stop sign, but with no indication of obeying it. They must not have seen the stop sign or Marcos coming. Either that, or completely ignored them both.

About the time the car's nose poked into the road, Marcos veered toward the middle of the road, hitting the brakes he kept in good check. Rather than honking like he wanted, he waved out the window to the vehicle who still hadn't stopped. The vehicle turned in front of them, and the taillights began to disappear up the road.

James clung to the roof's handle, petrified as his eyes were glued to the road. "What the heck?" His breaths came in spurts. Anger darkened his tone. "Why didn't they stop?"

Marcos could only laugh. "Get used to it. You will see a lot of that." He coaxed the jeep back up to speed. "That is the reason you must pay attention for everyone, including others. They get used to pulling out and no one coming. It's nothing personal, it's just what they are used to."

James shot Marcos a suspicious stare. "I have come to the conclusion you are as crazy as they are."

Now, how had he come to that conclusion when Marcos had just avoided a collision with another car? "Yep, I probably am."

Rather than dialoging with James about being crazy, he chose to watch a bulldog up ahead, trotting half in the road. He took his time passing it, making sure not to hit it. As the dog moseyed back up onto the curb, unaware of the danger just inches from his tail, Marcos pointed him out. "With all these dogs out here? A lot of them are friendly, and a lot of them will bite. Look at that bulldog up there. It just barely even looked. I have never seen a reaction out of it, but that chihuahua dog down there," he nodded to the house with the S-shaped driveway, "Will take your pants off. When I know by looking at a dog that it will bite, I tell people that I am not a chewy toy, I'm not a dog treat, and I'm not dog food. There is no reason to take a chance. If you do it, it's your fault for getting bitten." He hated it, but that's the way it was. "There are a number of carriers around here that have been bitten, some severely, even having to have repair surgery. You will hear me say that over and over. Don't take chances."

"I don't intend to." James shook his head with determination. "Not with dogs."

"Sometimes," Marcos followed. "The local dogs come up to the post office to harass people, maybe even bite them. A couple of the more prominent people have been chased into their vehicle, some bitten. We use to keep a Justin Case bar by the back door."

James' face twisted in confusion as it worked hard to riddle out what Marcos meant by that – just as he had with the special brownies. Finally, he gave up. "What is a Justin Case?"

Marcos grinned, wide. "*Just in case* we have to use it!"

"Oh." James breathed a half-hearted laugh. "Right."

Marcos relished in the fact that they were nearly at the point where they could go home. Not only was he bored with babysitting and being the one to initiate most of the conversation, but he was ready to be done with work. The days where the mail route ran late were getting to be too long. He was ready for a rest. The weekend – meaning Sunday – couldn't come fast enough. Knowing he was close to the end of the day made him happy enough to volley the conversation back and forth, as much as he could. "Like I have said. Some people are extra worried about their mail. Like the locked boxes in front of their house. I mean really, who wants your junk mail and bills? It's not likely someone is going to riffle through someone's mail and come up with money." He grinned, turning around. "Maybe in the 1800s and 1900s, but not now. Most of what comes in the mail is junk."

"Right? That's exactly what I've been thinking this whole trip!" James tossed his hand in the air. "Like that one house with a locked box! Like, seriously, dude?"

Like, seriously. Sometimes Marcos forgot what it was like talk to a teenager.

He propped his arm up on the window, glancing town at the weathered skin, having put up with numerous sun rays over the years. "Are you ready for your half farmers tan?"

"What is that?" James' eyebrow creased.

"Well, a farmer's tan is usually just an upper body tan or just the arms tan and everything else shiny. A half Farmer's tan is where you have one tan arm and nothing else is."

James glanced at Marcos. His nose wrinkled, and he hissed out a laugh. He shook his head. "Sure."

***

They were almost done. The end of the day couldn't come fast enough, and it hadn't either. James wasn't sure if it was just the training or if it always took forever like this, but he wasn't sure the paycheck was worth it. The longer the day stretched on, the more he entertained the idea of driving away forever at the end of the day. These people, man. They were paranoid. Rude, inconsiderate, and dangerous. How many times had they nearly gotten in a wreck...and it was only Wednesday. That Gene guy, the weirdo murderer Marcos had just handed off his phone to. And not only that, the sorting.

James had been sitting here, thinking of ways to get on the road faster so he could be done quicker, and decided that he didn't have to read the whole address. That is, until Marcos told him that thirty thousand residences might have the same number. So he'd have to read all the address, maybe even the town name, too.

Could this get any worse?

When he'd applied for a job in Gillham, he hadn't expected to be transported back in time 100 years, where DPS was nothing more than a nice acronym and a far-off dream, if that. How was he expected to get any of this done?

Boring. Long. Redundant.

James was exhausted. And to top it all off, Marcos must've thought he was his nephew or something from the way he kept force-feeding him unsolicited life lessons, about God, money, everything. James was tired. His eyelids dropped, heavy enough to be considered steel doors. He wanted food, a nice drink, and a good long nap.

More than that, he just wanted to be done.

Chapter 16

It had been hours. Hours of grueling, redundant work, hand in hand with babysitting, but Marcos finally reached the last box for the day. He didn't think about having to do it all again tomorrow, nor did he think about how little or much James had retained. He was just happy to be finished and savored delivering mail to the final box.

Which wasn't an easy one. Not with the box merely a stone's throw from the house itself. Marcos minded the front of his jeep as he eased up next to it. "This is one of a few disability boxes we have." He savored the moment of putting the mail in the final box for the day. Just like that, the lid was sealed. And, done. "He can barely walk with a cane. I typically take any package to his door just because he can barely walk, so he doesn't fall. Being nice and good to people goes a long ways."

James nodded. "I can see that."

Marcos was glad that he was finally starting to see that. It wasn't like he'd been hammering it home the past three days. "I got called out one evening about someone that couldn't get up off the floor." Leaving the mail route behind for the day, he urged his jeep to the speed limit, headed for the post office. "I knew he stayed drunk all the time. He kept lots of alcohol in the house. When I got here, I realized he was having a heart attack. We got him packaged up and sent to the hospital. The paramedic was yelling at him because he wasn't making sense." Marcos' voice fell accordingly, and he shook his head. "His buddy, who was also drunk, made the 911 call. I can't believe he realized something was wrong. He remembered nothing about the several days in there, including us getting there, or heart surgery. He has never drunk alcohol since. Yes, miracles happen." He spoke the confirmation out loud, partially to James, partially to himself. "He is a mess if you talk to him. He talks a little slow, but is funny. His old neighbor made whiskey, and I learned the basics of making moonshine and whiskey from him."

Interest drew James's eyebrow into an arch. He slowly turned to look at Marcos, almost impressed. "Why are you delivering mail? Wouldn't moonshine be worth more?"

"Sure," Marcos quipped. "But I don't want a cellmate named Bubba. I kinda like sleeping in my bed and seeing my wife."

"I would do it," James said in a clipped tone. He faced forward, eyes securely fastened ahead. It was funny how he could look ahead physically while saying a statement like that. Ironic, Marcos thought, that he could look ahead now, but not with his life.

Finding it something he could send James home with, he softened his laughter. "If you look ahead at the future, you can plan and save and be wealthy. It's the same thing with God; you have to look at your future because your future is what you make it."

A shadow crossed James' face.

"Another thing?" Marcos wasn't about to let it go. And it wasn't like James could go anywhere. He would not walk to the post office, Marcos knew that. "I have known a number of people that sold drugs and moonshine. None of them ever made it rich. Most ended up with cellmates."

"Sure." James's disbelief crossed this tone.

Marcos didn't want to let it go. When he looked at James, he saw a young kid, determined to cheat his way through life if he could, take the easy roads out and wind up on a harder one in the future. "You can't look at life day-to-day. You have to look at it long-term. Just like this work." Marcos gestured to the road. "You may see the worst of a lot of people out here. Seldom will you see their best, but it's not personal. Most of the time, they are having a bad day. There are some that are just not nice people here, but it's the minority. You will think a lot of these people are weird. Well, to them, *you* are weird. If you look long-term, you will see your flaws and theirs, and be able to know how to treat each one, even when they have a bad day. Most of the time, you will have very little interaction except when you are running late or someone is mad." At the words *your flaws,* James appeared to shut down even more. He crossed his arms and cleared his throat, clearly uncomfortable with the words of wisdom Marcos offered him.

"It's just like living for God." Marcos went on. "It's a long-term commitment. I will also tell you, I was your age yesterday, and that is how fast life goes. Be good to others, and do what is right daily, even when its not popular. If everyone else is doing something, it's not good in your personal life, or for God. Success is what you do in life, not dollars."

Not liking being preached at, James hardened his face and wouldn't even look Marcos in the eye. "Okay." He shut down the rest of the conversation.

Maros wasn't sure if he was planting seeds or throwing corn kernels against a brick wall. But at least he tried. That was all that mattered.

They pulled into the post office shortly thereafter. As Marcos turned the key in the engine, he turned to face James. Putting on his regular chipper tone, he asked, "Well, wasn't it better?"

James slowly brought his shoulders up to his earlobes. "I don't know, man. There are a lot of boxes, and the people are just different."

"Oh, now." Marcos laughed. "It ain't that bad. Just think! You might find the love of your life doing this." He tried tossing out the one thing James seemed to enjoy about his job. Meeting girls.

Not even that seemed to work. James wasn't very flattered or humored. He snorted. "I don't know about that."

Tension radiated off of him in waves. Not saying another word, Marcos let him pick up the mail they'd brought back with them and exited the jeep. It was one of the rare cool summer nights Arkansas granted its residents once in a while. The sun dipped low toward the horizon, promising a few more rays of light for the day before bidding the world good night. Marcos paused to take them in for a second, knowing that by the time he left the post office, they'd be gone.

James took no such consideration. He went to the post office and began the work of putting the mail away.

Marcos trailed after him, not engaging with any more conversation. He was tired of being the one to initiate it. But, at the same time, he didn't want to lose the kid. Sure, the first days were always bad. But if James established a habit of quitting, he'd never be victorious in life. One day, he'd regret that, whether he believed that now, or not.

Marcos sighed and faced him. "Is there anything you can think of that might make it better?"

"Yes." James barked, pivoting to face Marcos. "If it was DPS."

Marcos laughed as he carefully picked his options for what to say. *In your dreams?* No, that would ensure James would never come back. *Try telling that to the postmaster who doesn't care?* Too rude, even for him. Finally, he chose, "Well, they might do that, sometime."

"I mean now." James's angry stare didn't deviate from Marcos.

Of course, he wanted it now. Everyone wanted fast solutions. Unfortunately, that wasn't how life worked. "Well," all Marcos could do was end with a promise. "It will be better tomorrow."

"Yeah, right." Not bothering to hide his disdain for his job, James grabbed his car keys from behind the counter and slung them around by the lanyard until he received a palmful of keys.

As they began to lock up the post office, James didn't wait before heading for his car. "I'll see you tomorrow," Marcos called to him.

James did a half turn. His headlights flickered, flashing a not-so-promising light that indicated he'd unlocked his ride. "Maybe."

With that, he slipped into the front seat.

Then he was gone.

Marcos watched his car disappear and sighed. Along with the numerous members he had accumulated for his prayer list, he added James and sent up a prayer for him, right then and there in the post office parking lot.

Lord...help him see.

What else could he say? He may never see James again. He might. The kid might reevaluate just how bad he thought the day was, and come back tomorrow. He might not. Marcos wasn't sure if he'd see him tomorrow or not, but he had done what he could for the kid.

He was in God's hands, now.

About the Author

Marc Rosson is a Christian. He was born and raised in Southwest Arkansas. Both sides of his family moved to the state in the 1800s. He grew up very poor, made it through the 11th grade, and earned his GED. A jack-of-all-trades, he is a heavy equipment operator and has been a contract mail carrier for 16 years.

Marc was a volunteer firefighter and first responder for eight years. For five of those years, he was the fire chief and was responsible for building the department up to one of the top volunteer fire departments in the area, with new and updated equipment. In addition to this, he was also a fire and BLS Instructor. Marc is also a real estate developer. In addition to this, he is also a Christian film writer, producer, and actor.

He has volunteered and helped inmates, both in and out of jail, to get their lives on track. He has volunteered in the community in many ways.

www.ingramcontent.com/pod-product-compliance
Lightning Source LLC
Chambersburg PA
CBHW071438090426
42737CB00011B/1697